# THE WINNING DEAL

## For
## STUDENTS

Virendra Nath Kashyap

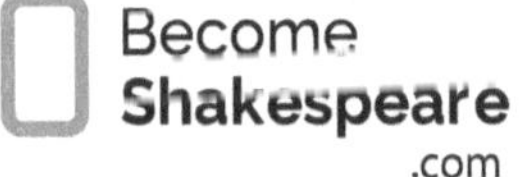

First published in 2021 by
BecomeShakespeare.com

One Point Six Technologies Pvt Ltd,
123, Building J2, Shram Seva Premises,
Wadala Truck Terminus,
Wadala (E), Mumbai - 400037
T:+91 8080226699



ISBN: 978-93-90543-14-4

# Dedication

This book is dedicated to the memory of Mr V.N. Kashyap. He started writing the book when we went into Covid-19 lockdown. He had completed the writing when he was unfortunately struck down by the virus. He lost his battle with Covid-19 in December 2020. We, the family, have provided some finishing touches to ensure this book is published. We hope this book provides you some help in your career journeys.

# Table of Contents

# Purpose Of The Book

While growing up as a child, many questions may come to your mind, sometimes about your studies, and at times about your life and career. However, I have seen that children go through their studentship like a block of cheese - eroded or nibbled from within because of the doubts and unasked questions during their study phase. At the end, they find themselves burdened with the weight of their unasked questions. This is but natural, because you are trying to shield yourself from **imaginary** ridicule. What will the teacher think if I ask this question? What will my fellow classmates think of me – a nincompoop? Why can't I find these answers myself? And you end up with unasked questions, not realizing that by doing so, you stunt your own growth in life.

Please do not let this happen to you. Do not curb the instinct to find the answers to your - **Who? What? When? Where? Why? & How?** at the right time or live with the doubts for life.

Finding answers to your questions/clarifying your doubts shows a healthy growth mindset.

In the early days, this scenario could be related only to your studies and sports that you were interested in. However, as you grow, these will be applicable to your life and career and also about your relationships in life.

My suggestion to all the readers: please read this book with the sole objective of achieving success through all the phases of your life. I am providing you with the tools to achieve success, but the only thing is - you will have to work hard. Work with my suggestions, imbibe what all I suggest here, and I am sure you will have more questions, and in turn, you will get all the answers to your - **Who? What? When? Where? Why? & How?**

All this, with the help of developing your soft-skills along with a strong base of core subject knowledge, will prepare you for a great future.

Wish you all the success!

# Preface

During my career, spanning 50+ years, I have done many recruitment-interviews. The positions for which I recruited included roles from very junior levels to the very senior levels, for both technical and non-technical and for various departments. However, the recruitment at the entry-level for the sales personnel, retail sales executives, BPO staff like data-entry and coders, always posed a greater challenge. This level of recruitment often brought out the gaps in the candidates' employability, from what we were looking for and what the candidates had to offer.

The gaps I am speaking about were mostly in the area of **soft skills** learning. It always stood out like a sore thumb because it was invariably lacking in the candidates. It's not entirely their fault though. In schools as well as in the colleges, until recently, there was no curriculum for training students in these soft skills.

Earlier, no one had ever spoken to them about the soft skills, and least of all, its importance in their lives. As a result, on many occasions, they lost the opportunity of getting the job to those who possessed these necessary skills.

This is what has led me to put this book together to help those children who, once they finish their 10+2 studies, will go to face admission interviews, and later appear for job interviews. I want them to be prepared adequately for the very first golden gate that will open up to their great career. My effort is to help such children learn soft skills and give them a greater chance of succeeding at whatever they plan to do in their careers by enhancing their employability quotient. This will give them the benefits of empowerment, self-esteem, confidence, and will overall improve their communication skills, resulting in being ahead of others.

A Stanford study, with a sample size of 10,000 successful people, was conducted to understand as to which of the two – domain knowledge/hard skills or the soft skills contributed to the success of the candidates. It revealed that the contribution of the domain knowledge/hard skills was 15% and the contribution of the soft skills was whopping 85%. Yet, what is the emphasis on the latter in the school/colleges? Almost negligible! 92% efforts in schools/colleges are put into teaching domain knowledge/hard skills and only 8% effort is put into **teaching** soft skills.

My effort through this book is to correct this problem.

**When and where does this soft-skills training start?**

I personally believe that the soft-skills training starts from the time the child is born, at the homes and from the families. Parents unconsciously begin to "teach soft skills" to their children with their own example. How do they treat other members of the family? How the family behaves in general?

Your empathy, your care for others, the respect you have for others, respect for time, the team spirit shown by family members in sharing house chores, etc. starts off the child with the learning of the soft skills, also referred to as Emotional Intelligence.

*Note for Parents and Teachers*

I also request parents, teachers, and school/college authorities to take more interest in imparting soft-skills training to their children. The benefits of learning soft-skills early in their life are far too many; it gives a head start to students in their lives. They learn better, achieve better results, get their dream careers, and earn better in the jobs that they pick up. This should be a good incentive to share your soft skills learning with your children and students. The Stanford study confirms my views.

## TAMAS/RAJAS/SAATVA

Here, I want to share a little about the three *gunas* (properties which are present in all the things in this world, including human beings). Learning to deal with these *gunas* improves our chance of success. These three *gunas* are: **Tamas, Rajas, Saatva**. They are present in different proportions in all of us. The variations in their proportional percentage gives us the unique personality traits. Let's see what it is.

**TAMAS** – inertia, laziness, depression, leading to darkness, destructive-suicidal tendencies.

**RAJAS** – action, passion, overreaction. (Ready to seriously harm someone!)

**SAATVA** – balance between the two, goodness, harmonious, constructive.

In order to be successful, we have to draw a balance between all the three *gunas*. At the spiritual level, it comes with practices such as meditation and yoga. However, you can master these three *gunas* in your daily life if you follow the self-development methods mentioned in this book. **This balance will lead to success** – you will learn to control your emotions, your behavior and your interpersonal/intrapersonal actions. Therefore, your aim must be to increase your **Saatva,** which provides the right balance of *gunas*. It comes with practice and I have included more details in the following chapters.

In life, you cannot afford to stay stagnant. If you wish to progress in life, you have to move *FORWARD*. Hence, you must acquire these skills to take a leap forward.

Also, I have a confession to make! The list of soft-skills that one can learn in his lifetime is very long; however, I have covered only a few of these. But I am certain that this will help you to start a wonderful journey while picking up knowledge as you progress.

*Have fun while you learn!*

*FORWARD!*

F – Find your strengths and weaknesses. Focus on success.

O – Organize your thoughts to align with your goals. Organize your day.

R – Read a lot. Research on what you plan to do and how others do it.

W- Work hard. Work towards your goal. Walk the talk.

A – Avail your opportunities. Act on what is right for you.

R – Respect your time. Stay ready at all times.

D – Derive the maximum from the present. Stay focused.

WISH YOU ALL THE SUCCESS!

# 1

# HOW TO MEASURE CHANCES OF SUCCESS?

## SWOT ANALYSIS

### Strengths Weaknesses Opportunities Threats

### *Your Journey Begins!*

While at school/college, you often wonder, "What should I do?", "Which career is best suited for me?", "How can I start planning my career path?", "What do I need to succeed?" etc. These are some of the questions for which all of us have sought answers at one point or another. It's not only during the school/college days that these questions keep popping up in our minds, but also at various phases/situations throughout our lives. After all, it is about our career and our personal life - the most important journeys that we embark on in our lives!

Whenever you embark on a journey, you take stock of the situation. Also, of the things and information that you will require to make your journey smooth. Your career path is the most important journey you undertake while you are still a student. In your case, it means, taking stock of where you are, what do you have by the way of education, what will you need while on your career path, who can help you in your decision making, how to take that most important step, etc.

To help you with this, I will introduce you to **SWOT** analysis.

To my mind, one of the most effective tools introduced for analyzing your present situation is the SWOT analysis. It was in the 1960s when a management consultant named *Albert Humphrey* invented it. Of course, it was initially intended to work out strategies for the corporates to compare their brands and products against their competition; however, it has found its effective application in various situations outside the corporate world. This is one tool that can help students to work out their own position at any given time in their academic career and, in particular, when they are preparing for an admissions interview.

**SWOT**

It's an acronym for: **Strengths Weaknesses Opportunities Threats**

It can be shown in a grid as follows:

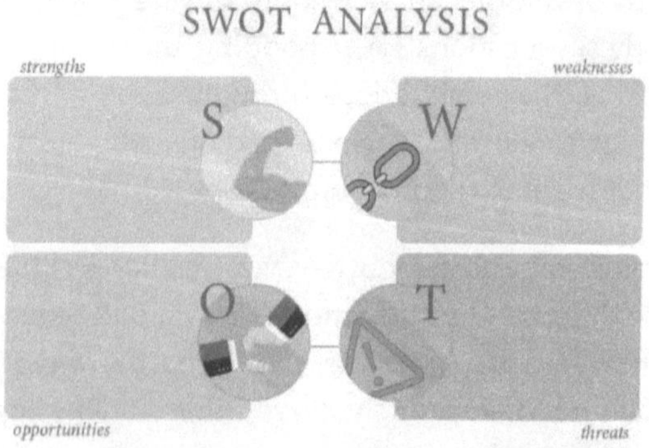

SWOT ANALYSIS

strengths

weaknesses

S

W

O

T

opportunities

threats

*Figure 1: SWOT Analysis template*[1]

---

[1] Created by Ms. Karishma Dewan

**Alternatively, you can create a grid as follows, for working on your SWOT analysis:**

| Strengths | Weaknesses |
|---|---|
| ■   .. <br> ■   .. <br> ■   .. | ■   .. <br> ■   .. <br> ■   .. |
| Opportunities | Threats |
| ■   .. <br> ■   .. <br> ■   .. | ■   .. <br> ■   .. <br> ■   .. |

This will help you to carry out a SWOT analysis. It is very simple; take a piece of paper and draw four squares or you may take four sheets of paper and draw a big square on each. Label the squares/ sheets separately for **Strengths Weaknesses Opportunities Threats** or in case of one square divided into four squares, the top two squares as **Strengths Weaknesses**, and the lower two squares as **Opportunities** & **Threats**. Now, in the respective squares, write down your strengths/weaknesses, and also write down what opportunities are available to you and what are the threats (obstacles) in your chosen career.

Once you do this the way it is described, you, at any given time, can know for yourself if you are pursuing the right career path in life or not.

You must also understand that **Strengths Weaknesses** are internal factors as they are within your control, but **Opportunities** & **Threats** are external factors as they are mostly out of your control.

Let me explain further. Suppose you are a student of class VIII in a good school/college. Very soon, you will come to a point in your education when you have to choose an academic stream – Science and Mathematics or Arts and Humanities? How will you choose to make your career a success? Your career will depend upon the subjects you study in school/college, and in turn, you follow them up for your college or post graduate studies. Are you not sure about what should be the combination of subjects that you shall have to study in the 10th to 12th class?

Sit down and do a SWOT analysis.

Under Strengths, list out the subjects that you know very well and enjoy studying. Then, list down your communication skills, your positive attitude, any excellence achieved in any of the subjects: they are all your strengths. Having been recognized as a leader of the class (as a class monitor, or a head-girl/boy) or being selected as a captain of a sports team, your friendly nature, your confidence, and ease with which you get along with others, enjoy working in a team, etc. are also your strengths. You may add your physical condition, team spirit, attitude, any achievements in the academics, co-curricular activities, or sports, etc. to the list.

Under Weaknesses, write down the subjects that you do not know very well at present, and it may happen that you do not enjoy studying them. Your physical health, your attitude, your behavioral limitations, being disorganized, etc. are all your weaknesses.  Under weaknesses, please also make note of all your negative habits like being lazy, procrastination, not being comfortable with any subject-not scoring well, not being a team person, lying habits, getting angry on small things, and so on, and being socially disagreeable, by and large.

Under Opportunities, write down the various career options available to any school/college pass-out, irrespective of what you wish to pursue at present. List down the complete elements. You can be a doctor, an engineer with all the different streams thereof, a playwright, a teacher, a scientist, a corporate executive, go into business, take CAT or other competitive exams, go for higher studies, join NDA, Police Academy, etc. The list is never-ending.

Under Threats, please write out the "obstacles" or the hindrances that you feel you face at present. Here, you will also list the subjects that are required for the career you want to pursue. But if you are weak in that subject or you are not studying the same, it becomes a threat till you work on it to overcome this weakness. The list will also include any of the physical attributes like weak eye-sight, loss of hearing, etc. because for certain services, you require 6/6 eye-sight and perfect hearing, or you are not as tall as required by the services/police recruitment boards. Even a high fee structure of the institution that you wish to join and you feel it will be asking for too much of your parents to pay for it, please write it out as a threat because you will have to find a way of overcoming this.

Make as exhaustive a list as possible and then work on it as follows:

CASE STUDY:

1. Suppose you are studying in grade VIII or grade IX. You want to be a doctor when you grow up. You will have to identify the college you would like to join for studying medicine. Find out the requirements the institute insists on for the selection process. What's the minimum percentage they require for considering you as a candidate? The

subjects that you will need to study and excel in, say, English, Bio-sciences, Math, Environment studies, etc. It is also required that you should possess good health as going through a medical college will demand a lot of your physical fitness. You will have to be observant, organized in your studies, have a good attitude for dealing with the faculty, and later with the patients, be good with your etiquette and very good with time management. Now, what does your SWOT analysis say? Match the requirement of the profession with the STRENGTHS that you have. Note down the WEAKNESSES and list out as to how will you overcome these weaknesses in the next 3 to 4 years. Then, go over the opportunities and threats, and once again, make a note as to how you will grab the opportunities and, if any, how you will convert the threat into an opportunity. Create an ideal grid, set goals to achieve success, and also set a time schedule for a review to stay on track.

2.  In the second example, assume you wish to join NDA or police academy to pursue a career in the forces or the police. Again, first and foremost, find out what are their basic requirements? A high grade in the 10+2 exam is definitely one of them. Your general knowledge, your positive attitude, your ability to think critically/analytically, team spirit, adventurous spirit, communication skills, interpersonal skills (in simple words – your likeability), emotional quotient and passion quotient besides your intelligence quotient are some of the other requirements that are a must for you to clear their selection process. Again, try to work on matching

these requirements, increase your strengths, set a goal to overcome weaknesses and remove the threats before you come to the stage when you actually have to face the test!

To both the examples, please add the interview skills. A good amount of study is devoted into building up knowledge about facing the interviews for success. So, start working on these straight away.

## BENEFITS OF SWOT ANALYSIS;

1.  Helps in strategic planning.

2.  Allows you to recognize and build on your strengths.

3.  Helps you to stay focused on available opportunities.

4.  Helps you to identify your weaknesses, so you can work on eliminating or reducing them.

5.  Allows you to plan in advance to overcome threats.

6.  Allows you to set realistic goals.

7.  Builds confidence.

## LIMITATIONS OF SWOT ANALYSIS

As important as knowing the benefits of SWOT analysis are, it is just as important to know the limitations as well. The limitations are:

1.  It does not offer a solution; you have to work that out yourself. It tells you where you are today; however, you have to work out on your journey requirements such as

mode of transport, the route you must take, pit stops on the way, etc.

2.    It cannot help you to prioritize your work plans.

3.    It throws up a lot of information, but you have to search for the right/useful information yourself as per your need.

**Usefulness – How to Get the Best Out of Swot Analysis?**

It is important to know and understand SWOT analysis and how useful a tool it can be for helping you to select the right course of studies. If you follow this, it will lead you to what you want to do and enjoy doing so! This is a very important mental build-up for success.

Once you have gone through the process of SWOT analysis, write it down neatly on a piece of paper or take a print if you can with all the parameters that are considered by you, and also include the goals that you have set for yourself. Then, you must prominently display it at a place where you can look at it periodically. Initially, look at it once or twice a day and thereafter, frequently as per your review goals. Once you start working on the parameters, you will notice the change in parameters depending upon the efforts put in by you in overcoming the weaknesses and also removing the threats. These may also change if you add more strengths to your grid. For instance, one of the weaknesses mentioned by you was, say laziness, and by working on it now, you are active in most part of your day. Please remove laziness from your list of weaknesses and add "active/alert" in the list of strengths.

Here, I would like to share a quote with you. I read this sometime back and it registered with me as a meaningful thought that should be kept in mind while doing SWOT analysis during your adolescent years, which you will need to do at various times.

*"Re-set, re-adjust, re-start, re-focus…as many times as you need to!"*-
*Anonymous*

This habit of SWOT analysis can stay with you as you grow. It will help you at all stages of life – even as a grown up!

2

# IMPROVING CHANCES OF SUCCESS

## SELF-DEVELOPMENT

*"You cannot dream yourself into a character, you must hammer and forge yourself one."*

*- James Anthony Froud*

Have you ever wondered how can you bring about self-development? How can you improve and develop your abilities and your capabilities? If you have, you are on the right track. In fact, anyone who wishes to succeed in life should always ask these questions to themselves.

Let me explain how you can bring about Self-Development. I am sharing two quotes for you to understand Self-Development better.

*"Personal development is the belief that you are worth the effort, time, and energy needed to develop yourself" - Denis Whitley.*

*"Every moment of one's existence, one is growing into more or retreating into less." - Norman Mailer*

These quotes should encourage you to start believing that whatever effort, time, and energy you put into your self- development, it will be worth it to make you a better person.

The decision is obvious; you want to grow more in your life than to be less! The drive for self-development impacts you on a daily basis; you are weeding out the negatives and developing positive traits in your life to make yourself a better person. So, your self-development is very important for succeeding in life. It will set you apart from the pack. You will outshine others in your sphere. Isn't that an achievement?

Please also remember - self-development is developing new skills, new traits, new habits in you, and self-improvement is improving on all of these aspects every day. Making your today better than your yesterday, and to make your tomorrow much better for you.

THE CHANGE IS THE CHALLENGE!

YOU CAN'T SPELL

*CHALLENGE*

*WITHOUT*

*CHANGE!*

If you are going to rise to the challenge, you'll have to be prepared to change.

*"Change is never painful. Only resistance to change is painful."* - *Anonymous*

ASPECTS FOR YOUR SELF-DEVELOPMENT

There are many areas in which one can develop oneself. However,

I am listing here a few "must" areas for you to focus on for your self-development.

PERSONA: Develop your personality to wear the mask of a good human being to start with. Develop the quality to like everyone; you must understand, develop, and show sympathy, empathy and honesty towards others. Help, understand and care about others, and develop team spirit A well-developed personality includes so many things like positive attitude, good body language, and excellent communication skills to name a few, develop these. This is also building your character to give your personality a strong foundation and building a strong persona for you. However, make sure it does not remain a mask, but it becomes a permanent you!

KNOWLEDGE:

*"To know what you know, and what you do not know. That's true knowledge." – Confucius*

Do not let the word "Knowledge" overwhelm you. Keep acquiring knowledge. Each experience in life adds to your knowledge. Without it, one cannot succeed in life; it's absence will make you dull. To grow in one's career, gaining as much knowledge as possible is important. Knowledge is also very important to shape our personality. It helps in perfecting our behavior and dealing with people – interpersonal skills.

TIME MANAGEMENT: You should develop time-management skills. Be punctual. This will always be of help to you in doing your things on time without any procrastination. You will stay ahead of others and finish the tasks better than others, and still have time to revise before it's due. This will also help you to do so many other things that you have always wanted to do.

DEVELOP RESPECT FOR TIME, YOURS AND OTHERS.

*"Personal development is a major time-saver. The better you become, the less time it takes you to achieve your goals." - Brian Tracy*

GOAL SETTING: Time management and goal setting go hand-in-hand. You set your daily goals, follow them at the time set for those chores, and voila, you have learned the art of time management. All goals are for your self-improvement! Let SWOT analysis be the basis of your goal setting, it will help.

ACADEMICS: It is a part of the subject KNOWLEDGE. However, it is important to remember the reason you are in school/college i.e. you need to focus on your studies. This means acquiring domain knowledge which forms the basis of your career. Keep improving your academic knowledge about the subjects you are studying. Stay focused, sit in the front of the class, pay attention to the teacher, and do not look at your watch (if you do, it means you are not interested in your development). Go home and revise the notes, read ahead for the next day's session. Help any of your classmates who may need help. Remember, teaching is the best way of learning. All of these will help you in your self-development.

Make it your objective to go through 6 levels of learning as per Bloom's Taxonomy-

- *Remember*: Remember what you learn for the first time.

- *Understand*: Understand what you learn.

- *Apply*: You should be able to apply what you learnt

- *Analyze*: Take it to the level where you can analyze the knowledge you have acquired.

- *Evaluate*: Know right from wrong, good from bad, etc.

- *Create*: With the knowledge acquired, take it to the level of creating something new.

You can apply the same principles for your sporting pursuits also. If you want to excel in sports, please follow the same regimen as you will be doing for your academics.

*"Change equals self-improvement. Push yourself to places you haven't been before."  - Pat Summitt*

## HOW DO YOU GO ABOUT IT?

The biggest change you can bring about in your life is Self-development. It is a Goal by itself that you need to set for your growth and success in life.

## SWOT ANALYSIS

- As explained in the chapter on SWOT analysis, firstly, find a quiet corner, sit down with pen and paper, and write down about your STRENGTHS AND WEAKNESSES. Make sure you are being honest about it. Do not exaggerate your strengths, and do not dilute your weaknesses. You must be truthful about your strengths and weaknesses. If you go wrong here, your total effort will be wasted.

- Direct this SWOT analysis towards your self-development.

- Also, please remember that most of us have our latent talents and abilities. Please try to learn to utilize them to the best. Here, your friends, family, or your mentor will be of great help to you in identifying these talents and your abilities. Sometimes, you are not even aware of your strengths!

- Match these efforts to capitalize on the opportunities lying ahead of you, as well as, overcome the threats ahead of you, if any!

- Now, you are ready to convert these into goals for self-development. Sit down and set goals for developing new skills and for giving up bad habits or what you have listed as your weaknesses, so as to stay on the path of self-development. This is like cleaning a hard disc, removing the garbage, and downloading the latest versions of applications for better functioning of your machine!

WHAT HELP YOU WILL NEED?

- You will need commitment. Self-development can come about only if you are committed to achieving it. It will need your 100% honest efforts.

- You will need a mentor. Your parents or any one of them, your elder sibling, your class teacher, can be your mentor. Select one of them. Seek their permission and share what you want of them. You'll need them to guide you in understanding your self-development goals, then help you in setting your goals, in assessing the progress you are making on day-to-day basis, and later, on a periodical basis. Anyone who understands your requirements and wishes best for you, can be your mentor.

## YOU DO NEED SOMEONE TO KEEP PUSHING YOU!

- You will need discipline. You will have to believe in what you have set out to achieve, and then, strictly follow your set plans. Have your mentor ensure that you do not go astray! Work on your daily goals. Stick to the time allotted for each activity. Find no excuses for not doing any of the activities you are expected to do at that time. You will not stop because you are tired; however, you will stop once the day-goal is met, or a landmark is reached.

- You will also need a reward system. If you reach a landmark as per schedule, reward yourself or your mentor could be requested to reward you on achieving the interim goals. This will boost your morale.

- You will also need to sacrifice. While pursuing your self-development goals, you may have to sacrifice a few things which otherwise may take you away from your goal, such as, not watching a movie when it is time for you to be practicing; giving up on playing games with your friends while you should be studying, etc. It may also mean material sacrifice like not going out to a restaurant for dinner, but, with the same money buying yourself the book you wanted to read for your self-improvement. Giving up on a new set of clothes but asking your parents to buy you tools you need to understand and carry out your science practical. (Good pair of runners for the sports enthusiasts.)

- Finally, you will need passion. You must want to improve yourself so much that you do not mind spending hours at it. Not only that, but you should also enjoy pursuing your self-development goals. All the time you are thinking about the goals, the means, and the methods of achieving the same to make it a success. You keep solving the math problem to make sure you are correct all the time, you write for hours to improve your hand-writing and keep improving on it every time you write a new page. Remember the example of Sachin Tendulkar? He practiced a particular stroke for hours together until he mastered it and enjoyed every moment of his practice. This is passion!

*"When you catch a glimpse of your potential, that's when passion is born."- Zig Ziglar*

IMPORTANT PRINCIPLE

$$< \, = \, >$$

This translates into the following.

<   Make friends with someone who is smarter than you. He can act as your guide and mentor. It could be a class fellow who knows more or better than you or could be your teacher. You can learn a lot from them.

=   Someone at par with you. Again, it could be a class fellow, a friend from another school/college, a sibling or a cousin, who is as knowledgeable as you. He will always act as a challenge for you to do better.

>   Someone who knows less than you and asks for your help from time to time. Remember, this too will help you in your self-development as there is nothing better in learning than teaching someone.

All of these will help you to succeed in your objective of self-development, and in turn, to earn life-long benefits.

*"Life isn't about finding yourself. Life is about creating yourself."* – *George Bernard Shaw*

# LOAD! AIM! SHOOT! ACHIEVE!

## GOAL SETTING FOR SCHOOL/COLLEGE CHILDREN

*"Don't be afraid to be alone - Goals are personal."*
*- Anonymous*

[2]Designed by Ms. Karishma Dewan

## DEFINITION OF GOAL

According to the dictionary, "GOAL is the end towards which effort is directed". Goals are dreams and wants. The only difference is that a goal is more specific.

In simple words, you come to school/college to learn and pursue the hard studies to achieve your aim and objective of your life. That's your goal.

**Look at it like this:**

Give a man a bow and arrow and tell him to "SHOOT!" His first response would be, *"At what?"* When there is no target, there is no purpose for shooting. He could shoot the arrow anywhere, and wherever the arrow ended up would be where the arrow ended up. Nothing much to it.

On the other hand, if you gave the archer a target and challenged him to hit the bull's eye – *everything changes*. You now gave him something to aim at, something to challenge his skills against, something to measure his progress with, and something that gives a *purpose* to all of his efforts. All by adding in a simple target –the GOAL!

Now, replace "shooter" as you. You are the shooter, aim/target is your goal, "bull's eye" is your specific goal and that's what I am going to explain to you so as to help you to become successful in life.

## THE PURPOSE OF GOALS

The purpose of your goals is to give you something to think

about; a definite direction towards your success in life. The most important thing is that you need to know about the goals, and you ought to have some.

## TYPES OF GOALS

There are many types of goals defined by time period related to the purpose of your life, like it can be your educational goals, behavioral goals, sports goals, etc. which I will explain later. Here, let me tell you about:

1.  Long term goals:10 years, 5 years, 1-year goals.

2.  Short term goals: goals for the next 9 months, 6 months, 3 months.

3.  Immediate goals: goals from 1– 30 days from now.

It's important to understand that your *immediate* and *short-term* goals can be **the parts** of your *long-term* goals.

To make you understand, I am going to suggest that you set goals for the end of your current school/college session. What you will do is, at the earliest, you will decide on your target for the whole of this year. This first step will be your *immediate goal,* which is identifying and setting the goal for the academic year. While setting the goal, you will also keep a check-date, say for 3 months later, to check the progress. This will be your *short-term goal.* However, the improvement in your grades by the end of the school/college term, which I believe will be your final goal in this exercise, will be the *long-term goal* for you. Follow the examples given above and set your goals according to the objective you have for your future career.

## DIFFERENT TYPES OF GOALS

There can be various types of goals in your life depending upon what you want to achieve. To name a few:

- Physical Goals: Your personal body care, health and fitness are physical goals. Reaching and maintaining a certain weight could be a goal.

- Career/Professional Goals: Where do you want to be after school/college finishes? What career do you want to pursue in your life?

- Financial Goals: By the age of 25, I want to be earning ...... per month, or, by the age of 30, I want to have ....... money as my bank balance, etc. could be your financial goals. I wish to own a house, worth. 2 crores rupees, by the age of 30, could be another one of your goals.

- Relationships & Family Goals: Socially, these are very important goals which one has to set in life, to be considered as successful. I want to be a dutiful child/I wish to be of financial help to my parents from the age of 21 / I wish to settle down with a well-educated (be specific about the qualification of the spouse), professional spouse by the age of 30!

- Self-development Goals: I wish to finish my PG qualification in management by the time I am 25 years old / I want to have a great personality / I should be a great public speaker or I want to be a great cricketer / athlete before I leave college / I wish to develop my confidence in the next six months. These objectives in life could be your self-development goals.

- Pleasure Goals: You must also set goals for your enjoyment when you grow up. Once every year, I want to travel to distant places for my enjoyment / I will take an annual holiday with my family to a different exotic place / I want to be able to paint well / I want to be an accomplished dancer / I want to be a playwright by the time I finish my college, are some more examples.

- Social Goals: As we are part of the society, we must also set goals to be useful members of the society. Your goal could be that I will be a responsible citizen and follow all the rules and regulations / I will pay my taxes as per the law / I will help the authorities in any which way they want me to do / or, I will train a minimum of three underprivileged children, at any given time, to help them earn a living / I will be a disciplined student in the class/school/college, I will work towards being selected as the monitor of the class by December this year / Head-Boy/Head-Girl of the school/college in the coming academic year. I am sure these goals will give you a purpose in life.

It's important to understand that you can set many goals simultaneously. Each serves a different purpose in our lives. One of the important skills that one must learn in life is to be able to multi-task but without diluting the effort for any of them.

As students, to start with, I am suggesting that you set the following goals. (You are free to select and set goals of your own choice).

1.  Physical goals: Set a time schedule and a measurable standard for your body conditioning. Each one of you will have different needs. Someone may want to gain weight, someone may want to shed weight, someone wants to build up stamina to be able to participate in games they like, etc. So, you will, under the advice of the elders and the experts, start working on it and also make sure that you set specific goals. However, make sure these are SMART goals - I will shed 2 Kg of weight in two months from now (set the date) or I will lose 5 inches off my waist in three months from today after I start my Yoga routine, etc.

2.  Study goals: Most important goals for you at the moment. Do a self-analysis, identify your needs, what subject/ topics you want to improve, and by when & how much? Take stock of your scorecard, say English 85%, Math 92%, Physics 78%, Chemistry 80%, Hindi 76 %, that's an average of 82.2%. You can now set goals either for an individual subject or on the basis of your average for the group of subjects. Let's say that you want to work to achieve not less than 85% in any of the subjects and overall a 90% score. Then, you set a time limit of six months from the day you have set the goal. Further, list down the preparations and time you will devote to each of the subjects to achieve your goals. Also, consider some bad days while doing the day goal, and get set to achieve the same. I am very sure that you will achieve the goal.

3.  Social goals: I am sure that you all want to be responsible students at your school/college, operate as a part of "the

class team" and together achieve more! So, set yourself the target of working as a team member. Sometimes, you will be a leader; at other times, you will be a member of the team pursuing the team objective. Social goals will also include your acceptability in the social group that you are a member of, your family, your friends, at your school/college/university, etc. You may have to give up on your anger, your impatience, your annoying habit of being late for any gathering, etc., if any.

> *"Our goals can only be reached through a vehicle of a plan, in which we must fervently believe, and upon which we must vigorously act. There is no other route to success."*
>
> *- Pablo Picasso*

So, let us understand the route and the vehicle of a plan.

## SMART GOALS

Just setting goals is not enough, we must set **SMART** goals.

What is this SMART goal? What are its five qualities?

**S – Specific:** Be clear and unambiguous when you're setting your goal. Don't leave room for guessing.

**M – Measurable:** Set a goal that allows you measurement toward your goals' progress.

**A – Attainable:** Ask yourself, "Is this realistic and attainable?" This does not mean it has to be an easy goal; it must have the challenge. If not, back to the drawing board!

**R – Relevant:** Create a goal with importance and meaning. Make sure that the effort is worth it to you. It meets your present requirement and is also a part of your long-term goal that you have set for yourself. As students, your goals will be related to your studies, etc. however; as you grow, the goals will change as per your requirements.

**T – Time-bound:** Commit to a deadline. Open-ended goals tend to lose the challenge and can go forgotten.

So, be SMART!

## BENEFITS OF SETTING SMART GOALS

- You know where you are going. It gives you a direction in life.

- You suffer less from stress and anxiety that are attached to being directionless. (Can a boat cross the river if you allow it to drift? You need a rudder to give it a direction.)

- You are able to concentrate on the subjects better.

- With the progress you make, you become more self-confident.

- Helps you to save time.

- Helps you to improve your self-image.

- Increases awareness about your strengths and weaknesses.

- Helps you to measure your progress.

- Keeps you motivated.

- Makes you feel happier.

This leads to success.

## PRINCIPLES OF SETTING GOALS

- First, do the SWOT analysis, sit in a quiet place, and reflect on what you want to achieve, and then select your goals.

- Select your goals carefully. Make them SMART goals.

- Write down your goals.

- Display your goals at a place from where you can read every day.

- Announce your goals to some other family member(s)/ class friends who you think will be of help to you and push you, if need be.

- Set cascading goals. Divide your long-term goal into an annual goal, a quarterly goal, a monthly goal, a weekly goal, and a day goal. YES, a goal for every day. This will help you to stay focused and soon, it will become your second nature. *No Matter How You Feel/No Matter How Busy You Are* – you have to meet your daily goal as set by you.

- Keep monitoring on a regular basis. In case of a deviation, set the course right immediately.

- Have an alternative plan for any contingency, a provision for any unforeseen condition.

- Giving up is not the option – remove it from your plans.

## TASK TO DO

Immediately do the following:

**DAY 1**: Your day 1 is the day you decide to set your goals. Select a quiet place where you can focus on this task.

Select an appropriate exercise book in which you normally write down your homework. This should stay with you as a reminder until the goals are achieved.

First, visualize what will be your goals. Write down a minimum of *THREE* of them, say, Physical goals, Study goals, and Sports/extracurricular activities related goals (Or any of the goals on your priority list.)

Write down each goal clearly. Follow the SMART rule.

Keep working on it during the day. Revise, if you must, however, by the end of the day, firm up on all the three goals. (Even if you need another day to work on it, please spend more time if need be, but do a thorough job.)

While doing it, you may ask yourselves the following:

1. I am good at…

2. I am bad at…

3. What I will improve?

4.   How will I make these improvements?

5.   What I will have to do, or I will need to achieve it?

6.   How will it be helpful for my career growth?[3]

It is important to remember the following if you really want to achieve your goal/s;

- You must own the goals, i.e. it is to your credit if you succeed, and it is your failure if you fail. Make sure it succeeds.

- You must control it. Any deviation in its progress, you should be able to take the corrective measures.

- Work on it faithfully. Give it your best efforts.

As Emma J Bell states, *"Dream It, Own it, and Work on it."* Without any of these, you will find that you fail in meeting your goals.

**DAY 2:**

For each of the set goals, prepare a timetable. Remember the cascading goals. Break down these goals accordingly. Most important will be - what will be the daily target for each of the identified goals. What I need to do every day to achieve my long-term goal? What facilities or help will I need for achieving the goal? List out, in detail, anything and everything that you may need for achieving the goal. This includes listing out the outside help that you think you will need as well as your own efforts.

---

[3] Adapted from Image Consulting and Business Institute (ICBI) course material

By the end of day 2, your roadmap for achieving the goal should be clear.

**DAY 3:**

Write down your goals clearly, preferably on separate sheets of paper in your notebook. For each of your goals, make copies and hang at vantage points: one next to the mirror in your room, one on the outside of your wardrobe, one where you normally sit down to study, one for your school/college bag - but keep it in such a way so that you can access it easily. Keep looking at the goals; You will need to do this till it becomes a habit and a part of your daily routine.

For every effort, there has to be a suitable reward. Think of suitable rewards for yourself as and when you reach an interim goal. It can be a break from the routine for a day, go watch a movie with friends, indulge in a feast with the family, or buy yourself the book that you have wanted to buy. It has to be something you desire.

Next; share the goals set by you with the family member/s, class fellow/s, or even the class teacher if it is related to your studies. Request for help, in case, you feel it necessary. Do not hesitate.

It is important that you have the right **F.R.A.M.E.** of mind while setting the goals:

**F.R.A.M.E. stands for**

**Fantasize:** As I have mentioned, dream your goals. Let it be a big dream, but make sure you are passionate about it and that you really wish to achieve it.

*"Don't let your dreams remain in your eyes; they will get washed with tears, settle these down in your heart where they will stay for as long as you want." - Anonymous*

**Reality:** Your grit and hard work will make your dream a reality. Work hard.

**Aim:** Aim high. However, let there be a reality between your wildest dream and the goal set by you - that becomes your aim.

**Method:** Select a method of pursuing the goals which you really wish to achieve. The path ahead should be worked out well. It is hard work or smart work for meeting your target. Iron out each prospect.

**Evaluation:** Keep evaluating as you progress. Let it not be the last step because you may have to do course correction on the way.

## START WORKING ON IT.

Please remember to include the following in the goals:

- *Immediate goal.* By following the above suggestions, you have already achieved your immediate goal.

- For monitoring, set *short-term goals* within the goals. Review after every three months or you can link it with your school/college calendar, but please, do not leave it open-ended. These will be your short-term goals. Finally, you are progressing towards your *long-term goal* which can be linked to the annual exams, if it is a school/college study goal or with the annual sports day if it is related to sports, etc.

**Do not forget to reward yourself for achieving your short-term goals!**

*"An unwritten want is a wish, a dream, a never happen. the day you put your goal in writing is the day it becomes a commitment that will change your life. Are you ready?"*

*-Tom Hopkins.*

**Please remember – YOU are the creator of your own destiny!**

There are a few other points worth remembering:

- *Start Small*: I am presuming that you are starting to set the goals for the first time. You may dream big, but for setting goals, start small. Break down your goals into doable parts as per your own capability to start with. Work with small increments. Gradually, keep taking the big steps so as to meet your deadlines as set by YOU! After all, from your house to the school/college, you walk one step at a time!

- *Be positive*: Have faith in your abilities and capabilities. Have a winning attitude.

- *Do not underestimate yourself*: This is very important to remember. You have the where-with-all to achieve your goals; just marshal the resources within you. Keep faith in yourself.

- *Be flexible*: Be ready to readjust your goals/or your efforts. If you find the goals set for the day is too easy, make it more challenging to keep the thrill in meeting your goal. At the same time, if you find that the day goal set by you is not possible and you have exhausted all options in trying to meet the day goal requirement, please ease out a bit rather than abandoning it altogether. So, it is important to be flexible.

## Do Goals Fail?

This is a very important question. The best of plans, most meticulously worked out, can also fail. Remember, how the Mangalyaan mission was aborted at the last minute? The team had gone over the details with so much of care, yet, they had to do the course correction at the last minute.

It will be prudent to know **Why Goals Fail? It could be due to one or more of the following reasons:**

- The goal was not written down.

- The path was not clear enough to follow with ease.

- All required inputs were unavailable at the time

- The goal was unrealistic or not specific enough.

- The commitment to complete a goal was missing.

- The goal was not shared with anyone else; hence, did not have the support of your team members when and where it was needed.

- The measurement/check systems were not built into the goal plan.

- Even after all of the set precautions are taken, an

unforeseen condition crops up!

- You did not build a reward system for yourself that led to demotivation and the goal was abandoned.

*However, I expect you to follow the principles of Goal Settings, follow the do's in a positive way, work on it with a passion – that's the* **WINNING DEAL.**

*"Don't stop when you're tired. Stop when you're done." - Anonymous*

# 4

## TOGETHER HEAVE HO; TO THE WINNING POST!

### WINNING TOGETHER

*TEAMWORK*

*"Alone, we can do so little; together we can do so much."*

*- Helen Keller*

It is now a well-established fact that the knowledge of soft skills is of great importance for growth in life. One of the most desired soft skills is – team building for **WINNING TOGETHER**.

Does it touch a chord in your mind? Does it tell you to develop the skill to work as a Team? I am sure it does.

Let me walk you through Team Building exercise with my 5 W's and 1 H.

**WHO:** It's YOU, of course! It's for your self-development. It's for your success in your life. You will see that working as a team helps you in meeting your objectives in life with a multiplier effect while allowing the team to succeed.

**WHAT:** It's a team-building skill. You can say, working as a team and winning together.

**WHEN:** "Now" is always the best time to start learning. There is no such thing as *later*!

**WHERE:** You may decide to start working as a team anywhere you may be. You can start by forming a team at home. Your classroom with your classmates is yet another team, as is the playfield or the library. The important thing is – to START. And it is here!

**WHY?** As it is already mentioned in the quote above, the purpose is to give your life a winning start; to win life's championship. This championship is an all-important event in your life. It helps you in meeting your individual as well as collective objectives, thereby reaching the goalpost ahead of others. Most importantly, it increases your potential to earn better. It gives you self-esteem which is so important to be living a successful life, for yourself and for the society. This is WHY!

**HOW:** This is an all-important question. Be a significant part of a team. Some of you may already be doing it, being a part of your school/college football/cricket/skating team or you may be a part of the dramatics/arts & culture team. However, you are also a team at home -your parents, grandparents, siblings all together are a team. You share chores at home, you sit together and discuss and sort out any problems. Teachers and students in a class can be one team as they create an environment for learning, so on and so forth. By abiding with the school/college rules, maintaining discipline at school/college, supporting the team effort in a sport is HOW you develop a team.

Here, I will explain some of the means and methods of winning together.

## THE BEGINNING

### What is a team?

A team is defined as a group of people, with common objectives and/or goals, pooling their skills, talents, and knowledge, with mutual support and resources, to achieve more effective results is a team.

Do you remember the old saying, "two heads are better than one"?

Team, Group, Committee are all a collection of persons; however, they are different from each other. How?

**Teams** embody a collective action arising out of task interdependency (depending upon each other)

- Members of the team agree on the goal.

- Members agree to work together to achieve the goal.

- They put in the effort to move in the same direction.

- Each member is viewed as having one or more important roles to play to successfully achieve the goal.

- There is less hierarchy within the unit than in most workgroups.

- The all-important TRUST is developed.

**A group** is a collective body of people, but they may not have a common goal.

**Committee** again comprises of a group of people, brought together for a specific objective; however, they may not agree and support each other's views.

The most **effective teams** arrive at decision through consensus by following a rational process that includes:

- Identifying the issue

- Setting a specific objective

- Gathering and analyzing the facts

- Developing alternatives

- Evaluating the alternatives

- Deciding and acting – implementing the alternative that is agreed upon

This also involves interpersonal interaction.

**So, are you ready to form a winning team?**

This will be possible only if

- You have selected the team members carefully.

- The team is committed to work effectively.

- The working atmosphere is positive, supporting higher production

- Each member is positive about contributing to the team effort.

- Each member is confident about the outcome. Each member enjoys the open communication, exhibiting high energy. The disagreement is also welcome and is handled without emotional conflict.

- Each team member has the trust of the other members to deliver just like/or better than the other.

**Key factors to successful performance of a team – S. C. O. R. E.**

Strategy - you have a plan to work on.

Clear roles and responsibilities.

Open Communication.

Rapid Response.

Effective Leadership.

So, to be a successful team, you need to have a fool-proof *strategy*. The road map should be worked out clearly and understood and agreed upon by all the members.

Next, is it clear who is going to do what? This means that each team member understands his *roles and responsibilities*.

To keep the atmosphere healthy, you need to have *open communication*. Each member has a right to give their suggestions, and the team can democratically decide the issue on merits. In *open communication,* you can disagree, rethink, and work out a solution which is acceptable to the majority.

It's equally important that once a decision is made, each and every member *responds to it immediately*. No inhibitions, no second thoughts.

Finally, it's good to have a leader in the team and he/she should be an *effective leader*. The leader should have the trust of all the members, capable of taking decisions in the best interest of the team.

This is the only way to SCORE over other teams.

**A FULLY FUNCTIONAL TEAM CAN...**

- Work together successfully

- Solve problems and reach decisions in a way that incorporates individual inputs and strengths

- Reach decisions through consensus

- Can adapt to change

- Achieve or exceed desired results

- Has trust and respect for each member and value their contributions

## RECIPE FOR A SUCCESSFUL TEAM

- **Commitment** to study hard and smart. This is your shared goals and objectives.

- **Clearly** defined roles and responsibilities

  - Teachers have to use the best skills of teaching you, while your role is to understand the subject being taught.

- **Effective** systems and processes include

  - *Clear communication.* Your teachers (leaders) are clear while giving the assignment and you make sure that you have understood the subject (instructions).

  - *Beneficial team behavior.* This means complete discipline like adhering to the school/college (team) norms.

  - *Balanced participation.* You accept the school/college (team) norms. Your teachers (leaders) show empathy for you. You also adhere to the time slots allotted for studies (for the task at hand) even if no one is watching.

  - *Awareness of the group process.* In a collective effort,

you share certain responsibilities while working towards your common goals.

- *Good personal relationship.* You show as much respect for the school/college authorities and teachers (organization) as you expect them to understand you and your point of view. Similarly, you respect the other team members for their contributions to the team effort, be it time and energy.

## EXAMPLE

Scene 1: You continue to study individually as per the norms till now. You will stay strong in the subject of your strength; but in the other subjects, you will remain average.

Scene 2: In your own class, your teacher is the leader. He/she identifies the strengths of each member of the class. Some of you are very good in English, some of you are good at math, some of you are strong in history & geography, yet others could be strong in biology.

Your leader, the teacher, assigns roles to each one of you as per your strength. Those who are strong in English will coach the rest of the class in English at a given time. They will be talking to you in English, correct your pronunciation, and maybe the spellings. Those strong in math will coach others in solving math problems and help you with practicing the same at any given time, also suggesting ways to do it accurately. Then, the batch of students good in history & geography will keep reminding you of the dates from the history lessons, sharing details about the geography; and finally, those strong in biology will help you with the biology studies, giving some hints on how to remember the details. Each person is helping the others as per their talent. As a result, the whole class is improving their scores in all the subjects. RESULT – better results for the entire class. This is one suggestion of teamwork.

## HELPFUL TEAM BEHAVIOUR

- Keeping peace and a collaborative atmosphere.

- *Being a friend*: After all, you are all classmates (members of the same group).

- *Being enthusiastic*: That's the best way of learning.

- *Giving opinions*: Share your thoughts; your suggestion may be the winning one for the team.

- *Generating ideas*: Keep looking at alternative ways of learning and delivering. There is always another way.

- *Initiating*: Someone in the team has to take the lead. Normally, it's the team leader selected at the time of team formation; however, at times it can be some other member.

- *Solving problems logically*: Gather all the facts, and then work on it like working on a jigsaw puzzle. Find the solution together.

- *Keep the humor*: Humor releases tension and nothing good comes out of working under tension.

- *Seeking approvals*: In a team, no one works individually.

You need to have the approval of the team.

- *Encouraging others*: Remember, it's a team effort. Carry everyone with you.

- *Eliminate toxic teammates*: You surely do not want to be pulled back by one negative thinker! Talk him out of the negativity or axe her/him.

- *Believe in yourself*: Faith can move mountains.

*Remember, if it was not a team effort, no railway lines could have been laid; no army could have won the wars without teamwork; Qutub Minar would not have been there; closer at hand – the Indian cricket team could not have been winning the matches as they are doing now.*

If you were to follow what I have explained here, you will become a part of a formidable team.

**T. E. A. M.: Together Everyone Achieve More.**

# 5

# DO YOU READ ME? YES...I READ YOU, ALL CLEAR!

## COMMUNICATION

*Teacher and the Taught!*

Within our society, we interact with others, day-in, and day-out, mostly by spoken words, and sometimes, we write to each other either on paper by a letter, or online, via email or WhatsApp, Instagram, or a plain message.

Just think, such a routine activity and have we ever given it a second thought as to what is it? Why we do it? What is the need? Yet we do it and we know very little about this action of ours, which is known as **communication.**

Human beings start communicating from the moment they are born. The mother's touch, the soft cooing of the parents, the lullaby sung to a child – all of it communicates love and affection. As you grow, you learn the art of communication in its entirety.

Be it your home, neighborhood, or your school/college, you communicate to learn the message of life. At school/college, you also learn hard skills. It's in the classrooms that you learn the basics of each subject that you study. Your teachers are committed to communicate the knowledge as it has to be understood to succeed in life. Your school/college anthem/hymn or the school/college slogan communicates the spirit of learning, of feeling proud of your *alma mater*, of bonding with the fellow students, and above all, inculcates the spirit of belonging to an institute which contributes to your growth in life. This is communication.

Through this chapter, we shall try and learn about this very important skill which, if mastered, goes a long way in making us successful in life.

Communication is the skill that helps humans to live together, work together, and bring joy to their lives. It serves as a basic need for humans to deal with each other being social animals! It communicates plain messages; it induces you to think; it communicates emotions, feelings, etc.

Quoting Wikipedia, "Human communication was revolutionized with the origin of speech approximately 500,000 BCE. Symbols were developed about 30,000 years ago. The oldest known symbols created for the purpose of communication were cave paintings, a form of rock art, dating to the Upper Paleolithic age."

Communication has always been the most significant part of human expression and interaction.

Communication is a vast subject. It has been studied very widely and on various aspects like its functions, need, advantages, etc. It has been the subject matter of various research projects - a lot has been understood and still the work is in progress!

**How did the first humans communicate?**

Early humans, all the way to the modern-day humans, have communicated in the same way as all the life forms. This covers about 500 million years' time, and the principal way had been through graphics, noises, and gestures.

**What was the first type of communication?**

The first means of communication was, of course, the human voice; but, in about 3200 BC, writing was invented in Iraq and Egypt. It was invented about 1500 BC in China. In India, the earliest deciphered epigraphy was found in the form of Edicts of Ashoka in the 3rd century B.C., written in a very early form of Brahmic script.

## How did communication change?

Communication has changed so much over the years. From speech to postal services, there are now telephones, cell phones, computers, and emails to text and video messages which make the way humans communicate extremely easy and fast. All these inventions have made life so much easier. Let's not forget that all the human senses contribute to the process of communication. So, it's as much a mechanical process as it is a biological process. The brain acts as the pivot for deciphering the messages (stimuli). It filters the contents for knowledge, emotions, biases, etc. A "meaning" is attached to the "message" based on which the brain sends signals to the sensory organs to respond.

Now, we come to one of the most important part of this chapter.

## What is communication?

We can understand communication under the following heads:

## DEFINITION

Already given a few descriptions above, but here are some more for better understanding.

The imparting or exchanging of ideas and information, between two or more persons by speaking, writing, or using some other medium is communication. The term "communication" has been derived from the Latin word *"cummunis"* which means common or give and take or mutual sharing. It is the art of transmitting information, ideas, and attitudes from one person to another. Education, with its correlated activities of teaching and learning, involves communication as well as reciprocal interacting between teacher and pupils, as a channel of realizing its objectives.

From "history of the word" (etymological) point of view, communication may be defined as:

(a) Sharing of ideas and feelings in a mood of mutuality.

(b) Interaction which encourages give and take.

(c) A process of sharing experiences till it becomes a common possession.

(d) A two-way process including feedback and interaction.

Communication is a need for a human being to communicate with his fellow-beings. It is an urge, and in the modem civilization, it is a necessity for survival.

## COMMUNICATION PROCESS

In order to understand communication, we must learn about the process of communication, which is explained through six steps:

**_The Six Step Communication Process_**

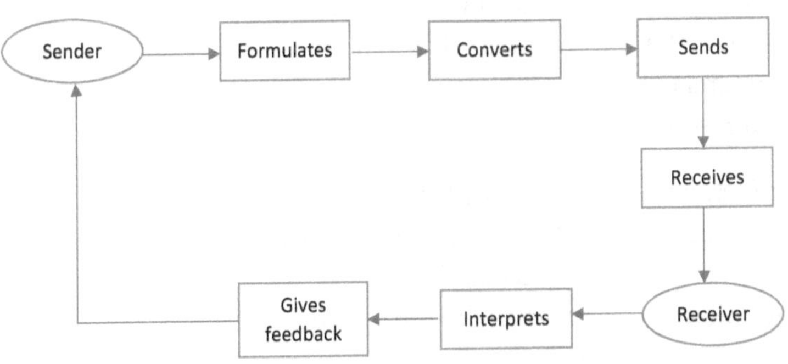


*Figure 2: The six steps of communication*[4]

[4]Adapted from Image Consulting and Business Institute (ICBI) course material

## Communication Process

The communication process consists of several components. Let's take a look.

A *sender* is the party that sends a message. You, of course, will be the sender. You will also need the *message* which is the information to be conveyed. You will also need to *encode* your message which is transforming your thoughts about the information to be conveyed into a form that can be sent, such as words.

A *channel of communication* must also be selected which is how the message is sent. Channels of communication include speaking, writing, video transmission, audio transmission, electronic transmission through emails, text messages and faxes, and even nonverbal communication, such as body language.

You also need to know the target of your communication. This party is called the *receiver*.

The receiver must be able to *decode* the message which means mentally processing the message into understanding. If you can›t decode, the message fails. For example, sending a message in a foreign language that is not understood by the receiver probably will result in decoding failure.

Sometimes, a receiver will give the sender *feedback* which is a message sent by the receiver back to the sender, generally as a reply/response to a message. However, it can even be in form of a question to clarify a point made by the sender.

The process of communication can be summarized as follows:

1.  The sender and the receiver both know the language in which the message is being sent.

2.  A sender encodes information.

3.  The sender selects a channel of communication by which they will send the message.

4.  The receiver receives the message.

5.  The receiver decodes the message.

6.  The receiver may provide feedback to the sender.

We have also taken into effect the *Background Factor* - on what basis the message is being formed; the *Need Factor* – what is the need for the sender to send the message; *Feedback* – sent by the receiver by means of a message, a question, or an affirmation, etc.

Being able to communicate effectively is perhaps the most important of all life skills. It is what enables us to pass information to other people and to understand what is said to us.

In order for the communication to be effective, we have to also understand the

## Communication Pyramid

**Communication Pyramid**

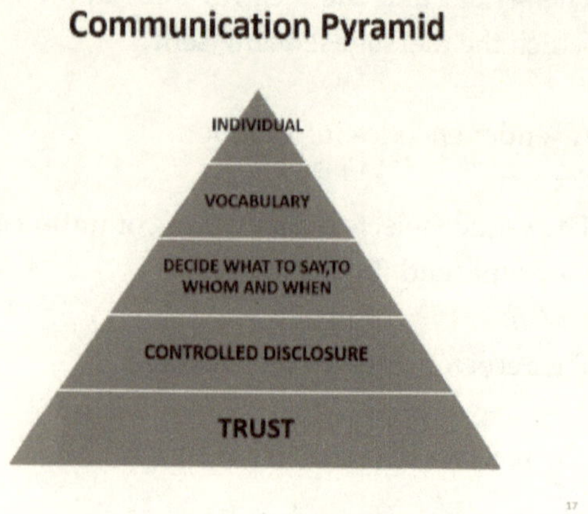

*Figure 3: Communication Pyramid*[5]

**Level 1 TRUST:** Trust is the bedrock of communication. You have to trust the sender. You have to trust your understanding of the language and decoding skill You have to trust the channel used for communication. Only if you have trust, you will receive the message in the way it is expected to be received. You have to trust the receiver for decoding the message faithfully/accurately as intended by the sender. You must have full faith in your teachers that they know the subject well – you will accept to gain that knowledge. Similarly, your teachers have trust in your ability to learn the lesson taught; so, the teacher will be able to finish the course in time and also may give a more detailed explanation of the subject.

[5]Adapted from Image Consulting and Business Institute (ICBI) course material

**Level 2 CONTROLLED DISCLOSURE:** You must also use control on your ability to trust the receiver and disclose what you feel is relevant for the person/situation. It should be just enough to convey the message intended to be shared. A teacher shares the knowledge based on the fact that the class can understand only to an extent at present; the details can be taught as the students go to the higher class. Can we teach trigonometry to class 2 students?

**Level 3 DECIDE WHAT TO SAY, TO WHOM TO SAY AND WHEN:** Can a teacher of class 2 students talk about the Pythagoras theorem? Or can the class of biosciences talk of astrophysics? The teacher has to know to what is to be taught to the class 2 children, and also that it is the bioscience knowledge to be shared with the class of bio students. Elsewise, the message will not get "received." In your school/college hours, with your friends, you talk about your homework and games, etc. in a lighter fashion, while with your parents, the same things you discuss in a formal manner. You can do back-slapping with your buddies, but not with your parents and teachers.

**Level 4 VOCABULARY:** Each language has its own vocabulary. We must develop it in order to communicate effectively between individuals of the same interest and similar background. Also, use the words which will be understood by the receiver. Each profession, each vocation has a vocabulary of jargon, which is understood within the circle; the others may not understand the same. CP for Connaught place, K for OK, CYA for see you, etc. are the phone message jargon that others may not understand.

**Level 5 INDIVIDUAL:** Each individual has their own understanding of the emotions/biases etc. as per their own experience. Each has their own behavior patterns, building up the character. To be effective in your communication with an individual, you need to know the other individual (receiver), use the knowledge about the earlier levels discussed above, and then communicate. There are different dynamics of communication which come into play while dealing with different subjects and for different occasions. With your best friend, you may show anger/indifference and makeup later; however, with the other class friends, you cannot take the liberty of being angry and ignoring them when they need you, because you do not have the same understanding that you have with your best friend.

Therefore, to be effective in communication, you have to understand the **communication pyramid** and encode your message accordingly.

**Mehrabian's Theory:**

Another aspect that we need to understand for effective communication is **Albert Mehrabian's Theory**. It has three elements as explained graphically in the chart below. Mehrabian's study establishes that the "words used" form only 7% of the communication process i.e. the vocabulary. The speech part of it – the voice tone mentioned in the chart which consists of the pitch, the speed, the emphasis, the pauses, etc. constitutes 38% of the communication process, and the rest, 55%, is the communication through the body language. Each of the constituents has its importance and must be developed as a skill to be effective at communication.

## Albert Mehrabian's rule

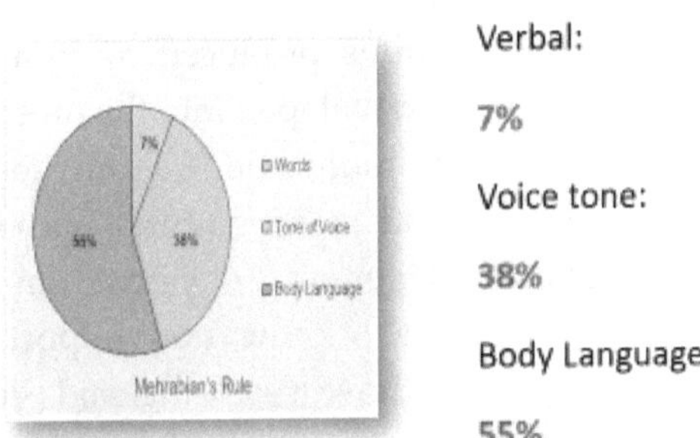



Verbal:

7%

Voice tone:

38%

Body Language:

55%

*Figure 4: Mehrabian's rule of communication*

I am sure you have understood different parts of the communication and the importance of each.

## What are the types of Communication?

In our day to day life, we communicate with different persons, on different subjects, and under different situations. As a thumb-rule, we accept four types of communication.

1.  Verbal.

2.  Non-verbal.

3.  Written.

4.  Visual.

Most of it has been dealt with above, however, we shall deal with each of these again, one-by-one.

1.  **Verbal communication:** It is the spoken word. Starting with the various sounds produced by humans over a period of time, it has developed into the most commonly used means of communication. From mere grunts, whistles, cat-calls, and some guttural noises, we have graduated to an intelligent way of verbal communication. Again, it is important to know, how important **what** is being said as well as **how** it is being said. Your speech, the pitch, the volume, the pauses, all contributes to make your message more effective. As per Albert Mehrabian's theory mentioned above, 7% of the communication is the spoken "words" and 38% is the "speech." Helping this cause, Alexander Graham Bell invented the telephone, carrying the verbal communication over vast distances through the electric wires. Even, the way the speaker speaks a sentence can change the meaning of the sentence as per the emphasis laid on a word.

    *"Words are free, it's how you use them, that may cost you." - Rev J Martin*

To understand the importance of stress on the word and its effect, let's take a sentence and then try and emphasize each word each time we repeat the sentence.

Statement: Harish will take me for dinner tonight.

(Highlighted words indicate the word on which the speaker puts special stress.)

i.   **Harish** will take me for dinner tonight. *Meaning* that it is Harish who is going to take me to dinner tonight and no one else.

ii.   Harish **will** take me for dinner tonight. *Meaning* that Harish will surely take me for dinner tonight; there is no doubt.

iii.   Harish will **take** me for dinner tonight. *Meaning* that Harish will take me for dinner tonight and not call for dinner or cook the dinner for me.

iv.   Harish will take **me** for dinner tonight. *Meaning* that it's only me who Harish will take for dinner tonight and nobody else.

v.   Harish will take me **for** dinner tonight. *Meaning* for dinner and not just for tea or a casual walk or so.

vi.   Harish will take me out for **dinner** tonight. *Meaning* again it is for dinner, not just going out.

vii.   Harish will take me out for dinner **tonight.** *Meaning* it is tonight, not on any other day or time.

See how the message is understood much more clearly by putting a little extra stress on the word you mean to convey your message to enhance the effect of the message.

2. **Non-verbal communication:** One part of the communication which has been the subject of research is the *non-verbal* part of communication. Initially, it was the corporates who laid emphasis on non-verbal communication. However, now it is being discussed with respect to all those who are in public view such as the politicians, the advocates, the doctors, the teachers, the trainers, and even the school/college and college students! Your appearance, your body posture, your hand gestures, listening skills, or eye contact are all a part of the *non-verbal communication.* Through all these, you communicate your attitude, your emotions, and generally send the stimuli for the receiver to decode and understand the message as per the receiver's interpretation (decoding.) Non-verbal communication enhances the effect of the message sent. You have to consider the following elements while learning about non-verbal communication.

i. **Proxemics**: The study of distance while standing close to the others or the science of territoriality. Here, we study about our *spaces.* You stand at a distance from the person you respect, persons with authority; however, you go close to the persons you love such as your parents and very close friends.

ii. **Haptic**: The study of touch. Handshake, a pat on the shoulder, holding hand or arm, a parental peck on the cheek, a tap on the knee for restraining you, etc. are some examples.

iii.  **Chronemics**: The study of the use of time. How you manage your time, how you respect other's time, how you structure your time are powerful communication tools. How you organize your study hours, your sports activities, your leisure time, and how seriously you take your school/college timings reflects your knowledge of chronemics.

iv.  **Chromatic:** The study of colors. These days, colors have been given positive or negative connotations in our social behavior. Like, it is common to wear black to indicate a sad occasion in the US, whereas in India we wear white for mourning. Similarly, tie colors have been given a meaning of respect and authority in our culture. For formal occasions, you wear a black or a red tie to indicate authority; yellow color indicates mutual respect for the others, etc. Red-colored dress for a woman indicates love and passion, light shades of the dress are preferred for a different reason. For men too, the color of your suit is indicative of different masculine messages such as respect for the others, asserting your authority, of a religious bent of mind, etc.

v.  **Olfatics**: The study of the sense of smells. Your parents ask you to brush your teeth in the morning to avoid anyone noticing bad breath with you, or they ask you to scrub yourself thoroughly while taking a bath so that there is no body odor when you come to the school/college. You are also asked to change your socks so that you do not go to the school/college with smelly socks, etc. When you are near someone and you speak to them and you have a bad breath, the other person gets a message that you do not follow oral hygiene, and that you are not bothered about the effect it can have on the others.

It can kill the communication. The same is true for body odor. No one wants to be close to another person who smells of bad body odor. Perfumes, scented powders, etc. can have a positive effect. It indicates that you care for the sensitivities of the others to the sense of smell.

vi. **Silence**: Even when we are silent, we are communicating. When someone else is talking and we listen in silence, we communicate to the other that we are listening to the other and we respect them. Or, in mid-sentence, if we go silent, we are indicating that we are reorganizing our thoughts to communicate effectively. Silence can be used for emphasizing on emotions also.

vii. **Sign language:** Since the early days, sign language has been used to communicate messages. The sign language of the Red Indians is one such example of communicating without the sound for communicating secret messages during battles or while hunting animals. Our civic bodies also use sign language in communicating to the masses, such as the road signs, the names of the roads or a sharp curve on the highway. Keep to the left, speed signs, etc. are used to advise the road users that you have to keep to the left and that the speed limit on this stretch of the road is 40/50/60 KMPH.

viii. **Appearance:** Your general appearance in the public also conveys a lot about your personality. Choice of clothing, accessories, color of the suit, of the tie, the shoes you are wearing communicates as to what kind of a person you are. You can be a respectful member of the society if you dress up soberly and appropriately for the occasion. Along with the clothes, your posture, your gestures reflect your confidence, your authority, and even the fact that you know what you are talking about. This results in your being taken seriously or not.

ix. **Kinesics:** The study of posture, hand movements, facial expression, etc. (The face is capable of approximately 2,50,000 expressions!) Anger, fear, love, surprise, joy, sadness shown in your facial expressions communicates as to how you should be treated at that particular time; thus, helping you to deal with the situation accordingly. Eyes, lips, hands, and the way you are standing, sitting, and various combinations of your hand movements, etc. communicate your thought process. It is very important to learn about the kinesics and develop the correct gestures, postures, facial expressions, etc. for effective communication.

x. **Oculesics:** The most eloquent part of your face is the eyes. It is commonly said that you communicate with your eyes even without speaking a word! Eyes reflect your state of mind very clearly. Added to that are the eye movements and the eye contact that indicates the joys and sorrows of a person to the other.

3. **Written:** With all the developments in the field of information technology, the computers, the smartphones where "messaging" & emailing has become the norm, the written word still remains a major part of our communication skills. For the students, in particular, taking notes in the class, doing your home-work and submitting to the teachers for corrections, sitting down

for your assessment tests, half-yearly and annual exams, a majority of you still need to write even if it's on the tablet or a note-pad. So, the written word remains a very important part of the communication skills. You must develop a good cursive handwriting with neat and clean strokes to enable the reader to read exactly what you have written. You must also adhere faithfully to the vocabulary and the script of the language in which you are writing. Wrong spellings, wrong grammar, inappropriate words at the wrong place and time can lead to disaster. It holds good for electronic messages also. You write out your message while sending an email, a text message, or any of the messages meant for any of the screens.

4. **Visual:** Since time immemorial, humans have been communicating through images, graphics, designs, etc. The best example is the rock paintings seen in caves dating back to the beginning of civilization. This helps human brains to retain and recall the signs while communicating with other human beings. Even today, the road signs, signboards, etc. are good examples of *visual* communication. For teachers, visuals are a very important tool for explaining things to the students in the class. In primary classes, the wooden cubes, triangles, squares, etc. are used in explaining the geometrical figures to the children; and then in senior classes, you show the visuals of plants, animals in their habitats in explaining the botany or zoology and so on. Have we not been using fingers to indicate the numbers? One finger

communicates one of anything, two fingers communicate two of the things, etc. The way we point our fingers is a visual message indicating the direction or a person or a thing etc. are the commonly used visuals in our daily activities.

Please develop all your senses and let these senses work through your day with proper communication. Observe the person, his personality, his behavior, listen actively to the message being conveyed, the words spoken, the pauses, even the silence in the sentence also communicates. Let your brain remain the pivot for coding and decoding the messages for you. Remove all the biases. This helps in developing strong *Interpersonal Skills* through understanding communication.

However, while learning the communication skills you have to be aware of the pitfalls which can lead to miscommunication.

**And what is that?**

**COMMUNICATION BARRIERS**

Communication can be a very complicated skill if not understood and applied properly. Since so many elements come into play in the whole process of communication, there are all the chances that there will be barriers to ineffective communication. Let's look at the *communication barriers.* These barriers can result in the message being misunderstood, misinterpreted, and miscommunicated in as much as being incomplete or unclear. There could even be doubts if it has actually been delivered.

**What are the communication barriers?**

- Physical.

- Language.

- Technology.

- Psychological.

Please read this in reference to the Flow Chart of Communication (Figure 2) above.

**Physical:**

- Noisy surroundings in an industry shed, football ground.

- Crowded place. You are in a bus, in a train, attending a party, at the cinema hall where there is inherent noise. It is difficult for verbal communication to take place.

- Unsafe place. It could also be due to your presence in an unsafe place where your mind is distracted because of the safety factor working on your mind.

- Uncomfortable place. At a funeral, we do not talk about the party - having fun together?

- Inappropriate time of the day.

- Listening. (*If you do not indulge inaccurate listening and effective listening, there is no communication at all.)

**Language: (*)**

- The two of you speak different languages.

- Use of jargons, acronyms such as your modern-day messaging.

- Use of difficult words, not understood by the receiver. (*Communication and miscommunication.)

- Use of incorrect/inappropriate words.

**Technology:**

- `Modern means of communication are not available.

- Bad connection (phone, internet, etc.)

- Inaccessibility, remote area.

- Channel chosen is inappropriate.

**Psychological:**

- Cultural influence. (*Cross cultural communication – In West Asia, it is common to touch each other; however, in Europe and Japan, it is not welcome.)

- The perceived bias of others.

- Stereotyping. (*Assumptions and presumptions! You will receive only what you are expecting to listen, you have assumed what the answer has to be, and it gets presumed even before a word is said.)

- Values in life

- Life experience

- Education or lack of it

- Emotional state.

We must make sure that for the communication process to go through safely and effectively; hence, we take care to avoid these pitfalls.

## HOW HAS COMMUNICATION EVOLVED?

In conclusion, let us understand how communication has evolved over the centuries. How human beings have had an interactive, participative way of a meaningful life. Let's go back to the history of communication, as already mentioned, in brief in the beginning.

The earliest means of communication recognized is through cave paintings. Cave walls were the "screen", the canvas at that time. This is approximately 173,00 years back.

*Picture 1: Ancient cave painting*

We have excavated and found paintings, inscriptions, and sculptures. When we look at these, you get a feeling that communicates a message. The message of joy, ecstasy, anger, sadness, etc. and it's perceived by the right hemisphere of our brain which is wired for feelings.

As we progressed, about 5000 years ago, we have evidence of Hieroglyphics. These are pictures in a sequence, like you have words in a sentence. The 'writer' drew pictures in a sequence to convey a thought, an event, and now, we use both the hemispheres of our brain to understand the message, i.e., left brain for the logic and the right brain for the feelings. Each picture is like an act in a theatre. You have to decipher the meaning!

*Picture 2: Ancient Egyptian Hieroglyphics*

Then, came the writing as we understand today. It started around 3500 years ago in Egypt and Iraq. The Phoenicians developed an alphabet and they wrote in an angular fashion. As we have informed earlier, in India, the earliest evidence are the Ashoka edicts written in Brahmic fashion.

*Picture 3: Ancient tablet carving and inscriptions*

This is the beginning of writing and reading of a message, as it is today. Using a definite alphabet, a predictable vocabulary emerged, and each language developed its own grammar. As a result, we could write a message, we could read a message and we could speak out a message to communicate with other human beings. This started the art of writing books and manuals for posterity. The communication thus emerged to be understood from one generation to the next through the books and edicts.

The language has evolved from mere graphics and designs to words and sentences; from writing on the cave walls to paper and parchments and canvases! The purpose solely remained to communicate.

A new dimension was added to the way we communicated – the voice for verbal communication when Alexander Graham Bell (along with Thomas Watson) invented the telephone, the means of transporting voice over electric wires. His idea has remained one of the most useful inventions ever.

Over the years, life carried on. We all mastered the art of communication through pictures, paper writing (letters, books, newspapers, magazines, etc.); through spoken words via telephone, radio, public speaking, class-rooms, etc. graduating to multidimensional means such as movies, TV, theatre, etc. With the entry of world wide web, Google, etc., there is a paradigm change in the way we communicate. The small screens have become the new cave walls; and there are new alphabets and a new language for use through the Instagram, Facebook, Twitter, WhatsApp, YouTube, with their own vocabulary.

Emojis are the new alphabet; each emoji communicates a whole message, and it depends how much you understand the new language. In fact, your whole brain is exercised in reading the emoji language.

Keep communicating intelligently, whatever the language be used, after all, staying connected with the society is the factor high on the longevity of your life.

Effective communication leads to success, so master the art!

6

# OPTIMIZE TIME; LET GO OF STRESS!

## TIME & STRESS MANAGEMENT

*"Time is free-but it's priceless.*
*You can't own it-but you can use it.*
*You can't keep it-but you can spend it.*
*Once you've lost it-you can never get it back."*
*-Harvey Mackay*

**T     I     M     E**

Today   **I**   Make (It.)   Easy

It means that if you do today's work today itself, your life becomes easy!

These are the traits of TIME. The most precious commodity that we all have is TIME, and it's perishable. What's with you today cannot be carried forward, so do your today's work today itself.

God credits your day with 86,400 seconds every day. How many seconds out of these 86,400 seconds you effectively utilize? You need to really sit down and tabulate. It's also important to know that any left-over seconds cannot be carry forwarded to the next day! It's just like the drop of water in the river; once it flows past you, you cannot catch it, ever.

Yet, most of us do not pay time the attention it deserves. Especially as students! Because at that age, we are not aware of its importance.

Just sit back and think about it, where does the time go? I am providing a list of a few of the activities of your day which can be the *time wasters*. Now, compare how many of these apply to you.

**WHERE DOES THE TIME GO?**

1. One most important time waster is procrastination. How many times do we keep postponing things?

2. You allow others to hijack your time.

3. You do not know how to say no.

4. Do you invest time or spend time?

5. Do you always do things at the last minute?

6. You are always complaining about a lack of time.

7. You do not understand the difference between urgent and important.

8. How many times you redo things because the first time you did a shoddy job?

9. You do not learn from mistakes and keep making the same mistakes.

10. You treat every work as on priority with the result that

the actual important works get neglected.

11. You do not strategize the most efficient way of doing things.

12. Time and motion are not studied; and as a result, you end up wasting time, duplicating the effort.

13. You do not club similar tasks to save time.

14. Doing something which pleases you more rather than the important tasks.

15. You do not anticipate things; you react to it.

16. You keep searching for things because you are disorganized.

17. You do not reflect on the days' progress; half of the things are not done.

18. You get overwhelmed easily with the result; you become unproductive.

19. You do not believe in preventive maintenance; you wait for the breakdown.

20. You do not address small problems before they become big.

21. You are indecisive; you keep going backward and forwards.

22. Are you productive while waiting for someone?

23. Do you settle for excellence before you achieve perfection?

24. You stress over things you cannot change.

25. You buy time by sleeping less; hence, you get fatigued and become less efficient.

26. Your to-do list is overloaded, more than what you can attend, resulting in shoddy work.

27. You do not reduce clutter and throw out the junk.

28. Allow distractions to sidetrack you from getting your main tasks done.

29. You do not allow yourself any downtime.

30. **Are you aware how you spend your time? If you are not, you are wasting your time.**

These are a few of the things we do, knowingly or unknowingly, that leads to this major loss of time. At the end of the day, we say, "How time flies!"

TIME and STRESS go hand-in-hand. If we do not finish a task in time, we stress! If we finish the task too early and have nothing else to do, we stress! We are not skilled to do the job; we stress. We shall cover all the reasons for stress later in this chapter.

Let's look at TIME first.

Time can be categorized into two types:

**Fast time** – When we're absorbed in an activity which we enjoy and are fully absorbed.

**Slow time** –When bored with the activity or having a bad time. For example, when waiting for someone and the person is late.

This brings us to the most important aspect of time – **TIME MANAGEMENT.**

Time management has five main aspects where the first four interconnect and interact to generate the fifth – results.

- *Planning & Goal setting.*

- *Managing yourself.*

- *Dealing with other people.*

- *Your own time.*

- *Getting results.*

**The essential good time-management habits are:**

- Know where the hours, minutes, and seconds are going.

- Stay focused on achieving the end results.

- Work on defined priorities.

- Schedule time for important issues.

- Delegate routine tasks and ensure that people take responsibility for doing them.

- Confront your own indecision and delay.

- Take the stress out of your work – learn to enjoy your work.

Putting the same thing in the words of leading experts, learn the art of smart time management

## SMART TIME MANAGEMENT:

- **S** – Schedule time, keep track of time.

- **M** – Make time for even small unpleasant jobs.

- **A** – Allot time as per the need of the job so that it takes the right time.

- **R** – Ration time; don't be lavish, otherwise the job gets stretched.

- **T** – Take time from others - delegate, so that you have more than 24 hours with you.

To help you with this, let's look at **The Eisenhower Decision Matrix**

Dwight David Eisenhower was a general in the US Army and he became the 34th President of the United States from the year 1953 to 1961. He is credited with the Eisenhower Matrix which he used for various activities and especially for TIME MANAGEMENT.

# The Eisenhower Decision Matrix

|  | Urgent | Not Urgent |
|---|---|---|
| **Important** | **Do**<br>*Do it now.* | **Decide**<br>*Schedule a time to do it* |
| **Not Important** | **Delegate**<br>*Who can do it for you?* | **Delete**<br>*Elminate it* |

*Figure 5: The Eisenhower Decision Matrix*

The matrix says, divide your tasks into four quadrants:

1. "Important" and "Urgent" tasks.

2. "Important", but "Not Urgent" tasks.

3. "Not Important", but "Urgent" tasks.

4. "Not Important" and "Not Urgent" tasks.

If followed correctly, it helps you in managing your time to its best, and also helps you to avoid wasting time on the non-essential tasks that don't even need to be done and would be considered a complete waste of time by most people. The quadrants are explained as under:

1. **Quadrant 1 - DO - "Important" and "Urgent" tasks.** These receive the highest priority level and should be your primary focus to complete as soon as possible (mostly on the same day). *Also known as the quadrant of Urgency.*

2. **Quadrant 2 – Decide - "Important", but "Not Urgent" tasks.** These are the long-term goals and tasks that are important, but don't have a firm deadline yet. You should schedule them in a timely manner, doing the most urgent ones right after you've finished everything from the "Do" quadrant. *Also known as the quadrant of Quality.*

3. **Quadrant 3 – Delegate - "Not Important", but "Urgent" tasks.** These tasks are the ones you can delegate to other professionals if you must, but only after your first and second quadrant tasks are completed. *Also known as the quadrant of Deception.*

4. **Quadrant 4 – Delete - "Not Important" and "Not Urgent" tasks.** The tasks are placed in the "Delete" quadrant because you should eliminate doing them. *Also known as the quadrant of Waste.*

In which quadrant you spend most time will determine how well you are managing your time. You are most productive in quadrant 2 - the quadrant of Quality. You must spend more time there.

There are other studies also done on Time Management, and one of these I wish to share with you is **Stephen Covey - 4 waves in Time Management.**

Stephen Covey works with the quadrant to help you manage the time effectively. He has come up with his four waves in time management.

1.  **Notes & Checklist**: Have a to-do list and keep checking on it.

2.  **Calendar & Appointments**: Follow the time schedules.

3.  **Prioritization**: Beware of the urgent and important jobs.

4.  **Self-Management**: Stay organized. De-clutter your mind and office.

To optimize on your time, also do the cascading time management.

- Have a yearly overview plan.

- Monthly plan

- Weekly plan

- Daily plan

It's important to understand that in the cascade, the time span keeps decreasing; however, the complexity of planning increases. Therefore, it's very important that you give an in-depth consideration while arriving at your cascading time management goals. If you do your daily tasks properly, it will take care of the weeks, and this will help you with your annual plans without losing any time.

Overall, what you need to do to be good at managing your time well is

- Have a great planning system and use it.

- Have a great planning system and use it.

- Take on realistic goals and schedule accurately.

- Do not over commit.

- Set and agree on priorities – Urgent v/s Important.

- Control your documents, workplace, and the use of the phone.

- Do not procrastinate. You cannot plan for it.

- Learn to say NO.

- Build-in time for personal development.

## ADVANTAGES OF TIME MANAGEMENT

I am sure you have an all-important question in your mind – What's In It for Me (WIFM)? The answer is

- You optimize the use of your time.

- You take control of your life.

- You stay stress-free.

- You focus on important things.

- You will make good decisions.

- You can finish the task as per the schedule and efficiently.

- You gain in your self-confidence.

- You are close to progress and success.

- You earn the respect of others.

- You effectively use the 86,400 seconds that God gives you every day!

Like a flowing river, time keeps flowing. To a river, you can build a dam to hold the water; however, I am afraid there is no such mechanism whereby you can hold the TIME for later use. It's perishable. It's now or never.

Set your priorities. Work toward your goals. Achieve your dreams. Make yourself happy. You can do it! Your time is ultimately yours and yours alone; make the most of it. Make every second count.

To help you understand the importance of TIME, I quote Julius Sevilla:

*"Time waits for no one, Time stops for no one,*

*Your excuses will not slow down time,*

*Your indecisions will not delay time,*

*Your complaining will not stall time,*

*And your regrets will not turn time back!*

*So, don't waste your time in anger, regrets, worries, and hate,*

*Because Time will not turn back and cry with you,*

*It's time to let go of the past, and stop worrying about the future,*

*Your only Time is NOW!*

*So, make sure you spend your time with the right purpose,*

*With the right deeds, with the right emotions,*

*With the right thoughts and with the right people!*

*Time flies…that's a fact,*

*But you can always spread your wings and soar with time,*

*And navigate life, the best that you can.*

*Remember, you will never pass this way again…...*

*Make it count!*

*Time, do what it does……Keep moving!"*

## STRESS MANAGEMENT

### What is stress?

Stress is the physical and psychological response to harmful or potentially harmful circumstances. It is a state of severe physiological and physiological tension, a non-specific response of the body to any demand. It is dominated by worry, anxiety, fear, which makes it difficult to cope with.

Stress is the "wear & tear" that our minds and bodies experience as we attempt to cope with our continually challenging and changing environment.

You can liken it to a rubber band. You pull the rubber band to stretch it to its limit. Beyond that, it will break. However, a qualified stretch on the rubber band is like a challenge in your life. If you take it positively, then it is a challenge otherwise it is a stressor. Later in the narrative, we shall talk about the benefits of stress in life.

Another definition: $S = P > R$ Stress occurs when the pressure is greater than the resource.

**How do we know that we are under stress?**

Worry, tension, tiredness, fatigue, fear, elation, depression, anxiety, and anger are some of the symptoms which indicate that the person is under stress.

Under these circumstances, you must not judge a person without knowing the "stressor/s" which are influencing her/his behavior. Here, the stressor is the cause of the stress.

**FACTORS CAUSING STRESS**

1. **EXTERNAL STRESS FACTORS**:

- *Physical Environment* – Bright light, Noise, Heat, Confined spaces, etc.

- *Social Interactions* - Rudeness, Bullying, Bossiness, Reprimand, Aggression by others.

- *Organizational* – Rules & regulations, Deadlines,

- *Major Life Events* – Birth, Death, Marriage, Exams, Loss of Job,

- *Daily Hassles* – Class tests, commuting, technical breakdowns

2. **INTERNAL STRESS FACTORS:**

- *Lifestyle* – Excessive caffeine, Lack of Sleep, Overloaded schedule, excessive workload, makes a demon of the class work/homework, taking things lightly.

- *Negative self-talk* – Pessimistic Thinking, Self-criticism, Over Analysis.

- *Mind Traps* – Unrealistic expectations, Taking things too personally, Exaggeration, Rigid Thinking,

- *Personality Traits* – Perfectionist, Work-alcoholic, "My Way or Highway" thinking.

To go through your life peacefully, you have to understand the stress, and also how to deal with it. Most of the stress we experience is often self-generated. Your attitude in life, your approach in life, your mental build-up - all help you to deal with stress. If your attitude is negative, you will feel the stress even if it is not there. Similarly, your biases in life will stress you without there being a need for it. One person's joy can be the mood destroyer for the other. You need to know how to deal with stress. Recognizing that we create most of our own upsets in life is an important first step in dealing with stress.

Stress response is controlled by the Endocrine System in our body. Demands on the physical or mental systems of the body result in hormone secretion (Adrenaline, Testosterone). Body responds to the endocrine secretion with increased pupillary dilation, perspiration, increased heart rate with increased blood pressure, rapid breathing, and muscle tenseness with trembling. Imagine a situation where you are confronted by a ferocious animal. Your heart starts beating faster, you start sweating, you may empty the bladder subconsciously, you may lose your voice, etc. That's a reaction to stress caused by fear. As students, you have to look out for the following to avoid going under stress.

- *Physical Symptoms:* Changes in sleep patterns, indigestion, fatigue, dizziness, headaches, general aches & pains, sweating, trembling, tingling hands and feet, faintness, breathlessness, missed heartbeat, etc.

- *Mental Symptoms:* Lack of concentration, memory lapses, difficulty in making decisions, confusion, disorientation, panic attacks, etc.

- *Behavioral Symptoms:* Appetite changes, eating too much or too little, leading to health issues, increased intake of alcohol & other drugs, increased smoking, restlessness, fidgeting, nail-biting, etc.

- *Emotional Symptoms:* Bouts of depression, impatience, fits of rage, tearfulness, deterioration of personal hygiene, and appearance.

All of these have the following Social Manifestations:

- Experience a sense of isolation

- Suffer from loneliness

- Frequently nagging others

- Lack of intimacy

- Lack of trust

- Social distancing – not going out with friends and relations

## Benefits of Stress

- It's difficult to even think of the benefits of stress. However, by controlling the stress and stress levels, we achieve more! The friendly stress before the exams or a presentation triggers the need to prepare well. Without that stress, maybe, we will tend to take things easy and not do as well in the exams.

- Stress makes you ready for the events to come.

- Pre-warned is pre-armed; that's what stress does.

- If you learn to deal with stress, it becomes your friend. It will prepare you to deal with things and situations better.

## STRATEGY TO DEAL WITH TIME & STRESS

## ABC strategy for Time

**Awareness –** It is important to be aware as to how are we utilizing our time, if your time is leaking. Be aware of your seconds and minutes; use your time effectively on the important jobs. Further, we have to be aware of what is urgent, what is important, and what is essential. Your routine of personal hygiene, your diet, your exercise are the essential jobs in your life. Studying, self-development, improving your behavior, etc. are the important jobs; those of the jobs if you leave till the end become your urgent jobs.

**Balance -** We must learn to strike a balance between important and not so important jobs which demand our time. We must minimize the time spent on the non-essentials and concentrate on the important tasks. Learn to stay in Quadrant II of the Eisenhower matrix.

**Control -** Though time is ours, yet we cannot hold it for eternity. So, the best thing to do is to control it. Set goals: daily goals, weekly goals, and your quarterly and annual goals. Make sure you spend less time on the non-essential jobs, taking care to do your jobs timely.

**ABC strategy for Stress**

As Time and Stress are interlinked, by adopting a similar ABC strategy for stress management, you can stay happy in your life.

**Awareness –** Be aware of the causes of stress in your life. You know your body and your attitude in life, so it is important to be aware of the stressors and take preventive action.

**Balance –** Certain stresses are "essential stresses" like the stress before the exams, stress before reaching the bus-stop. These stresses motivate you to do your tasks in time. However, there are non-essential stresses which affect your body and mind profoundly. You have to develop a balance between these stresses to stay happy.

**Control –**To stay stress-free in your life, you have to learn to control the stressors. It could be a person, a thing, an event, or act of another person which is adding to your stress. How do you control it? Dealing with it directly, moving away from it, or learning to deal with it. All comes with self-control.

*"One of the best pieces of advice I ever got was from a horse master. He told me to go slow to go fast. I think that applies to everything in life. We live as though there aren't enough hours in the day but if we do each thing calmly and carefully we will get it done quicker and with much less stress."*

*– Viggo Mortensen*

7

# OPTIMIZE TIME; LET GO OF STRESS!

## ATTITUDE

*"There is always a choice about the way you do your work,
even if there is not a choice about the work itself."*
*- Stephen C. Lundin*

We have often heard people talking about some other person, saying "…he has an attitude." Or "he has a positive attitude," or "he shows attitude while dealing with his juniors." In fact, not always do we understand what it actually means. Suffice it to say that it's a very important part of our personality.

**What is attitude?**

Attitude is our willingness, or the lack of it, to react, respond, approach, and act in different situations, tasks, environments, to different kinds of people, or life itself – it's a state of mind.

Talking simply, attitude determines how we deal with people, tasks, and situations in our lives. When a teacher gives an assignment to the students, generally, there are two types of reactions from the students – a few students will say "How nice! We get to learn new things!" and the other set of children will say,

"How boring! There goes our free time." These reactions depend on their attitude towards learning.

## FOUR TYPES OF ATTITUDE

- **Positive Attitude**

- **Negative Attitude**

- **Neutral Attitude**

- **Sicken Attitude**

**Positive Attitude**: This is one type of attitude in organizational behavior. It is expected of the students that they will develop a positive attitude in general. They will always look at the brighter side of things. For instance, a teacher gives a difficult problem to solve, a positive student will say "How nice! It's a challenge and I will solve it to add to my learning." You have just been given the results of your mid-term exams and you find that you have not scored so well. For a positive student, the reaction can be "I am happy with the results, I still have time to improve on my learning before the final exams, and I surely will."

**Negative Attitude**: In a similar circumstance, a negative student would react something like this. On being given a difficult problem, he says, "What do I learn from these difficult problems? These are out of course." Or "Our teacher wants to help only one or two of our class fellows to show off with these difficult problems, the rest of us can do nothing except to fail." To the other situation, their reaction again will be negative, "Our teacher is giving us low marks on purpose, and I do not think I can improve any further." One must always avoid negative attitude,

**Neutral Attitude**: With this attitude, a person shows that he is not bothered about anything. He tends to ignore the problems of life. He usually says, "I don't care if someone fails or secures top position. I will follow my own pursuits. What's important for me is that my position should not get affected."

**Sicken Attitude**: This is the most damaging of attitudes. Here, a person only thinks negative for the others. In a race, they would expect the other competitors to suddenly fall sick and get out of the race. In reality, they wish all the worse things for the others, be it the family or friends.

So, it's important to have a positive attitude in your life. Because of this positive attitude, some people can break records in the same set-up in which others break themselves.

When you change the way you look at things, the things you look at change. In the classroom, when you are given a problem to solve, you look at it positively and say to yourself that it is easy, and you will be able to solve it without a doubt. However, if you look at the same problem with a negative attitude and you'll say that it's very difficult and you will find it difficult to solve. See, how critical is your attitude in contributing to your success?

Let's look at the three elements of your personality to understand the whole perspective. Within your personality build-up, you have

**ABILITY** – helps you to decide "what to do?"

**MOTIVATION** – will give you the reason "why must you do it?"

**ATTITUDE** – will let you know "how well" you do it.

**Here we shall be talking about "how well" you do it:**

**Attitude.**

First and foremost, you have to **Choose Your Attitude.** To actually choose how you respond to life, not just react, you must be intentional. When you get up, decide who you want to "be" today. Moment-to-moment awareness is key. Ask yourself throughout the day, "What is my attitude right now? Is it helping the people who depend on me? Is it helping me to be the most effective?" Self-affirmation plays a strong role in developing your attitude.

There is always a choice about the way you approach your STUDIES, even if there is not a choice about the studies itself, you have to study to progress in life.

Your attitude is affected by three elements

1.  **Environment**: The environment in which you grow up will have a strong influence on the attitude you develop in life. If the environment at home or school/college is generally a happy one, you grow up feeling happy towards all situations. Everyone attends to all the chores happily, without grumbling. Even during adversities, you saw your parents, family react calmly, positively towards the crisis and they dealt with it without fuss. Your attitude will also develop to be positive in such ambience.

2.  **Experience**: Your experience with the things, people, and places will influence your attitude. Your class teacher teaches you a subject in a very friendly way with lots of enthusiasm, and in a helpful manner, your love for the

subject will develop and you will enjoy studying that subject, which also adds to your experience in that class and your attitude will always be positive. You will start loving teachers in general. Or, if a teacher has been very critical of your work, and your experience has been that he is always grouchy, your attitude towards that person and that subject will remain negative.

3.  **Education**: It's not just the school/college course studies. This also includes the learning through books you have generally read for yourself. What you read earlier on in your life also affects your attitude. Add to that your experience in life; the wisdom will determine your attitude in life.

Part of our attitude is EGO, let's look at that.

## EGO

A tiny part of your attitude is EGO; however, it's a significant part of the attitude. If the whole continent is the attitude, then a small city is the EGO. However, you cannot ignore the city as it adds to the WHOLE of the continent.

*"When you allow your EGO to control your thoughts, everything you believe becomes an illusion." - Rusty Eric*

One of the biggest reasons why ego is your enemy is that it keeps you out of touch with reality. Your ego is what prevents you from hearing critical but necessary feedback from others. Ego makes you overestimate your abilities and worth, and under-estimate the effort and skill required to achieve your goals.

For instance, in a competition, one of the champions has a positive attitude towards winning and the other has a bloated ego and an attitude. The first, down-to-earth champion says, "I will try my best to win" and he wins. The other person says, "No one can beat me" and comes across a stronger competitor and loses! That's what ego does to you!

One has to learn to avoid EGO to be a part of your attitude and your personality.

For EGO, let me say this: *Eeee...let it GO!*

Back to Attitude, a question arises: **Is there a magic formula for improving attitude?** [6]

No, there is no magic formula; however, there are ways – The Power of Eight.

1. **The Power of Visualization**

- Have a vision for yourself, for your growth.

- Have faith in yourself. Believe in your pursuit.

- Learn to *fantasize!* This way you practice your vision often.

*"I thought continuously of the day I would walk free. I fantasized about what I would like to do." – Nelson Mandela*

2. **Self-Motivation**

- People can inspire you, but you *alone* can motivate yourself.

[6]Source Mr. Ashish Ranjan, Horizon Group

- Find your motive. What gives you the energy to do a task or live a productive life?

- Be realistic with your motives.

3. **Affirmative Attitude Talk**

- Maintain a conscious, continuous, positive internal dialogue.

- Do not *ignore* your inner voice.

- This constant reminder wires your brain and affects your behavior.

*"Every morning I look in the mirror and ask myself – if today was the last day of my life, would I still do the same set of things that I will do today? If the answer to this is NO for many days in a row, you need to change your approach to life." – Steve Jobs*

4. **The Power of Words**

- What we speak reflects about what we think.

- Greet people in a positive way.

*"One kind word can change someone's ENTIRE day." - Anonymous*

5. **Enthusiasm**

- Enthusiasm/energy is not a physical condition, but a state of mind.

- You have this gift – use it more effectively.

- Passion ignites greatness.

6. **Humor**

- You lighten up life with humor.

- The more of humor you have & the more you spread it, the lesser will be the stress in your life.

- If you laugh, you make others laugh too.

- Laughter creates positive energy.

*"Nothing is more contagious than a smile." - Anonymous*

7. **Positive Thinking**

- It means that everything is possible.

- Positive thinking.

- Positive actions.

*"Positive Will & Skill can help you succeed in life." - Anonymous*

8. **Psyche yourself up for success**

"I am the greatest! I am the champion! I am the greatest! I am the champion!" This is how Muhammad Ali, one of the greatest boxing champions in the recent times, used to psyche himself even when he was an unknown boxer. This can help you succeed in life against all odds.

It's important to know that every student should have the following attitude

- Politeness, patience

- Willingness to learn

- Hardworking nature and perseverance

- Good reading habits

- A sincere student should stay away from social media as a time pass and also the mobile other than using it for its important functionalities.

- Respect for time, yours, and others

- Very good behavior towards others

- Being helpful

- Ever smiling

Here, I wish to share with you a beautiful message which one of our late cricketers, Mr. Raman Lamba (Life Coach), had penned and is still relevant.

*"INCREASE YOUR HAPPINESS QUOTIENT*

*Happy people do things differently to increase their level of happiness. These are the things that we can start doing from today to feel the effects of happiness in our lives, because no matter what part of our life's path we are currently traveling on, these "happiness attitudes" will always be applicable.*

1.  ***ATTITUDE OF GRATITUDE****: - When you appreciate what you have, what you have appreciates in value. So basically, being grateful*

*for the goodness that is already evident in your life will bring you a deeper sense of happiness.*

2.   **ATTITUDE OF OPTIMISM** - *Winners have the ability to manufacture their own optimism. No matter what the situation is, one who is strong and steady will always find a way to put an optimistic spin on to the situation and move on. For them, failure is only an opportunity to grow and learn a new lesson in life.*

3.   **ATTITUDE TO AVOID COMPARISON** - *Comparing self to someone else can be poisonous. If we are somehow "better" than the person we are comparing ourselves to, it gives us an unhealthy sense of superiority. If we are "worse" than the person we are comparing ourselves to, we usually discredit the hard work that we have done and dismiss all the progress that we have made. What I have found is that the majority of the time this type of social comparison does not stem from a healthy place. If you feel called to compare yourself to something, compare yourself to an earlier version of yourself.*

4.   **ATTITUDE OF KINDNESS** - *Performing an act of kindness releases serotonin in your brain. (Serotonin is a substance that has tremendous health benefits, including making us more blissful). Selflessly helping someone is a super powerful way to feel good inside. What's even cooler about this kindness kick is that not only you will feel better, but so will people watching the act of kindness.*

5.   **ATTITUDE TO NURTURE RELATIONSHIPS** - *The happiest people on this planet are the ones who have deep, meaningful relationships. Studies show that people's mortality rates are doubled when they are lonely. There is a warm fuzzy feeling that comes from having an active circle of good friends with whom you can share your experiences.*

6. ***ATTITUDE TO FORGIVE*** - *Harboring feelings of hatred is horrible for your well-being. You see, your mind does not know the difference between past and present emotions. When you "hate" someone, and you are continuously thinking about it, those negative feelings are eating away at your immune system.*

7. ***ATTITUDE TOWARDS COMMITTING TO YOUR GOALS*** *- Being wholeheartedly dedicated to doing something comes fully equipped with an ineffable force. Magical things start happening when we commit ourselves to do whatever it takes to get somewhere. When you are fully committed to doing something like you have no choice but to do that thing. Counter-intuitively, having no option - where you cannot change your mind - subconsciously makes humans happier because they know part of their purpose.*

8. ***ATTITUDE TOWARDS SPIRITUALITY*** *- When we practice spirituality or religion, we recognize that life is bigger than us. We surrender the silly idea that we are the mightiest being ever. It enables us to connect to the source of all creation and embrace and accept the supreme energy.*

9. ***ATTITUDE TOWARDS CARE TO YOUR BODY*** *- Taking care of your body is crucial to remain happy. If you don't have your physical energy in good shape, then your mental energy (your focus), your emotional energy (your feelings), your spiritual energy (your purpose) will all be negatively affected.*

10. ***ATTITUDE TO LOVE SELF*** *- If you cannot love yourself, then you definitely cannot be at peace with others also. Do not blame yourself for the mistakes made in the past nor have unreasonable expectations out of you."*

It is seen that it is important to have a positive attitude in life. This alone will spell success for you during the study days as well as in later days in your life, in your career.

## How Can You Tell That You Have a Positive Attitude?

1. *Positive Thinking*: "I am going to have a great day today", "I am going to learn a new lesson today", and "I will be joining my school/college team for winning the football championship"! What do these statements say? Very clearly, they say that you have a positive attitude because you are thinking positively. It will also show in your personality as you go through the day today.

2. *Smiling*: The smile on your face tells a lot about your attitude. Your positive attitude is reflected in your smile. You smile when you are at peace with the surroundings and yourself.

3. *Gratefulness*: If you are grateful in your life, you will create an atmosphere of gratefulness. You are grateful for the bread on your plate. You show gratefulness for the good parents/teachers/friends. You show gratitude for even small happenings in the day like, "bully smiled at me and made up with me after the altercation". Being grateful for things that others take for granted such as lovely parents, nice house, good school/college, helpful teachers, etc. It gives you an internal calmness that adds to your personality.

4. *Helpfulness*: You are always helpful. Only those who are generally satisfied with their lives think of being helpful

to others. Great attitude!

5.  *Kindness & Care for Others*: You show kindness to the others, to those who are weaker than you, those who are in need, you worry about the other person's difficulties, and you care for their wellbeing; you come to their help.

6.  *Enthusiasm:* You show enthusiasm for your studies and other activities you are involved in. This brings in a positive energy around you. The whole class will feel it and it will get carried to the others.

7.  *Energy*: You have a passion for studies, and you approach it with energy. This again is shown in your personality.

8.  *Control Anger*: You do not get angry at anything since you have a balanced approach towards everything/everyone.

9.  *Good Listener*: You are an active listener. Your teachers will like you. You will also learn better that adds to your success. This is an important part of your personality, so, develop this habit.

10. *Respect*: You have self-respect and others respect you for all these qualities. You get along with other persons very well; your work gets done.

11. *Respect for Your Body*: You maintain good health. You take control of your personal hygiene to keep yourself healthy. A healthy body leads to happiness.

12. *Nothing Annoys You*: You are in control of your emotions. You do not get angry at others or in bad situations. You

have learned to deal with it with a positive mind as *anger* is the enemy of your mind and body. It affects your mind and body negatively which is counterproductive.

So, with a positive attitude, you ride ahead of success, and it will follow you for sure.

Make your choice, it's your **attitude!**

# 8

# LET'S CREATE A SPACE FOR OURSELVES!

## PERSONALITY DEVELOPMENT

*"Personality can open doors, but only character can keep them open."*
*- Elmer G. Letterman*

It is very common for us to refer to certain people by saying;

"He has a great personality."

"He has a magnetic personality."

"He has a very happy personality."

"He has a great presence."

"What a personality, so charismatic!"

"She has a charming personality."

The reverse of these that we normally say;

"He is so negative."

"He is always critical of everything."

"He never smiles; he is forever grouchy."

and so on.

Do you know what *it* refers to in a person? It's about his *Personality!* We are quick at forming an opinion about a person. We are labeling a person based on their appearance, their behavior, their attitude, all are parts of the personality of a person.

## WHAT IS PERSONALITY?

*"Personality is to a person what perfume is to a flower!" Charles M. Schwab*

*"Personality is made up of the characteristic patterns of thoughts, feelings, and behaviors that make a person unique." - Igor Balasanov*

While there are many theories, the first step is to understand exactly what is meant by the term *personality*. The word personality itself stems from the Latin word *persona* which is referred to as a theatrical mask worn by performers to either project different roles or disguise their identities.

Let's look at the three related words: PERSONA – PERSON – PERSONALITY.

PERSONA: We all have our *PERSONA* – we put on a different "mask" for our roles as a parent, as a child, as a student, at work as a worker, or as a manager. Some of us could be students, teachers, lawyers, doctors, engineers, etc. and our thought process, our behavior, changes with the role that we are playing at a particular time – that's our *PERSONA*.

*PERSON*: Next comes what we are: a *PERSON*. As a person, we are packed with bundles of emotions. This is a little more consistent than the *PERSONA* which can change as per the situation. As a person, we depict our mental build-up based upon the teachings, experiences, learnings, etc. and it develops into a fairly consistent behavior in our life. The value in our life and our character describes who we are as a person.

*PERSONALITY*: Derived from the word *Persona*, PERSONALITY is the visible part of a person. It's a combination of various traits of a person, all put together. Personality is made up of the characteristic patterns of thoughts, feelings, and behaviors that make a person unique. In addition to this, personality arises from within the individual and remains fairly consistent throughout life. It is both felt and seen.

The part, that is visible of us to the others, like the trunk of the tree in the picture below, is the personality. The roots, the part which is generally not visible to the others, are the values which govern our thoughts, and actions are your character which too is a significant part of our personality.

*Picture 4: The personality tree*[7]

[7] Created by Ms. Khushi Kashyap

Let us first deal with the visible parts of the *personality*.

For clarity, let's understand personality under three heads: The **A B C** of personality.

Here,

**A** stands for *APPEARANCE*.

**B** stands for the *BEHAVIOR*.

**C** stands for *COMMUNICATION*.

## APPEARANCE

When you first see a person, in the first few seconds (0 to 7 seconds), you form an impression about the person. This is based upon the first look, the appearance of a person. What is he wearing? How does he stand? What are his hand gestures, overall body language, etc.? These are all unique to a person and depict their personality.

### Your First Impression

*Attire* – What are you wearing. Is it appropriate for the place and the occasion and your calling?

*Posture* – How are you holding yourself: relaxed, standing tall with shoulders back, or are you slumped in the chair?

*Eye contact* – Solid with a "smiling" face or avoiding eye contact.

***Gestures with hands and arms*** – purposeful and deliberate or fidgety.

*Speech* – Slow and clear, well-articulated or incoherent and disoriented.

*Tone of voice* – Moderate to low or it is slang-bang.

This is your **Body Language.**

Most communication is 35% vocal and 65% body language (non-verbal communication). If you can combine good body language along with speaking, it can work wonders for you. The way you walk, sit, and talk, it's all included in the body language. Everything matters, and to be successful, you must undoubtedly master body language at its best.

Personality development makes you feel good. For everyone, personality development generates a sense of happiness in their mind. This makes you *look good, feel confident.* This is first lesson in learning and being successful.

## BEHAVIOUR

Another important aspect of personality is a person's *BEHAVIOUR.*

It means the way you conduct yourself in the society, within your family and within your immediate group of friends and relations.

Behavior is an action that is observable and measurable. It is what we see or hear, such as students sitting down, standing up, whispering, yelling, or writing. For example, a student may show anger by making a face, throwing a pencil, turning away from the teacher, crossing the arms, etc. We label them as undisciplined. A student who pays attention in the class, does their homework properly, we label them as a well-behaved student, a disciplined student.

## FOUR TYPES OF BEHAVIOR

*Optimistic. Pessimistic. Trusting. Envious.*

*Optimistic* and *trusting* are the ideal types of behaviors expected of students which leads to positive learning. Both relate to a positive state of mind. You can be optimistic if you think positive. Similarly, trust comes with positive thinking about the other person.

*Pessimistic* and *envious* types of behaviors are negative behaviors and can lead to deficit learning. You are always thinking of the worst to happen to you. You only say that today may not be a good day for me, or, instead of improving yourself, you keep feeling jealous of the other person's achievements. You feel envious of the other persons' popularity or their success in life which they may have achieved with a lot of hard work!

**What are the positive attributes of the behavior of a student?**

1. Discipline

2. School/college, classroom and playfield Conduct Skills

3. Observation Skills

4. Participative in Extra-Curricular activities

5. Strong Communication Skills with class fellows and Teachers- building relationships.

6. Commitment to Learning

7. Working hard.

8. Sense of respect.

9. Sense of responsibility.

Therefore, a positive, optimistic, trusting behavior adds to the student's personality.

## COMMUNICATION

We have now covered two of the three important parts of our *Personality*. *Appearance* is the first impression which generates an immediate response from the people we interact with, and then comes the *Behavior*. This too is an important part of our personality as it affects the others and they do notice it. Not only notice it, but they do also measure it - his behavior is *BAD!* He has *impeccable* behavior, etc.

Now, we come to the third part of our personality component - *Communication.* Communication is a vital function in our daily life and is a very important part of our personality. When a speaker walks onto the podium, after noticing their appearance, after the body language, the behavior, what is the next thing we take a note of? Their speech! The way they communicate the message, the tone and the pitch of their voice, what they communicate, what is their thought behind the message, so on and so forth. We associate it with their *personality.*

It is important to understand how communication becomes an integral part of the personality. Communication is a vast subject, that's why we have devoted a separate chapter on communication. Please refer to that chapter for understanding communication.

Now, let's define Personality based on communication. It can be defined as:

i.    A transactional process that involves the exchange of ideas, information, feelings, attitudes or belief and impression.

ii.    A process of passing on information and understanding, from one person to the other.

## Power of Speaking

Accepting communication as an integral part of the personality and by regularly practicing personality development skills, you can have effective communication. Personality development includes learning vocabulary, and also widening the scope of knowledge and thus helping you to *share your thoughts and ideas in a better way.*

It is more important for the students to develop the power of speaking in the early stages of their student days because it's going to govern their life in a big way later on. You need to develop a good vocabulary for the subject that you are studying, add to your knowledge by reading more than what is taught in the class, apply the knowledge to your daily life for solving problems, or sharing/conveying your thoughts to others.

Every language in the world has its vocabulary, its grammar, and its dialect. As mentioned earlier, only 7% of our communication is the words we use. The rest, 38%, is how we say it, what is the tone of your voice, how clearly you speak, when is the pause in your speech, and so on. Even that pause in your speech conveys a lot

We do say that a person is soft-spoken; it is a type of personality. Or, we say that he always talks aggressively; this is another type of personality. To emphasize a point, someone may use a lot of gestures; this is yet another type of personality. Based on all of this, you make up your mind as to the person being likable or disagreeable.

As students, effective communication helps you in building up your personality and it can be understood by following the rules, as given below:

*LISTENING:*

Do you know that while sitting in the class, you listen through your body?

1. EYES – Looking at the teacher talking.

2. EARS – Both the ears are ready to hear what is being said.

3. MOUTH – Keeping quiet, no humming, and no whispering. Keeping a smile on. Using it only for asking relevant questions.

4. FEET – Staying still, quiet on the floor.

5. BODY – Positioning yourself, facing the teacher.

6. HANDS – Quiet in your laps/on the side or taking notes.

7. BRAIN – Thinking about what is being said. Full focus.

8. HEART – Caring about the teacher who is speaking who has put in an effort to teach you.

Listening is very important in the process of communication. As a student, you have to know the five steps to better listening.

- **Receiving** – Become a SPONGE, absorb everything. The sender while sending the message has encoded a specific message for the receiver which, in this case, is you. Now, to understand the message in the manner as it is intended to be understood, you have to listen to the message and receive it properly. While receiving the message, make sure there is no *disturbance, you do not interrupt the speaker, and you do not rehearse a response till then*. The response should come after understanding.

- **Understanding** – Become a TRAMPOLINE – bounce the message and retain what is relevant. Again, the importance of understanding the message should not be lost on the students because unless you understand the message properly, i.e. you decode the message properly, it will not achieve its intended meaning. It must be converted to knowledge.

- **Remembering** – For a student, it is important to be able to remember what has been conveyed by the teacher in the classroom. Without remembering, you shall not be able to understand the lessons being listened to. *Identify the fundamental points; make yourself familiar with the fundamentals* for a proper recall at the appropriate time. It is implicit, *recall* is equally important.

- **Evaluating** – Once you have heard the lesson, you have understood what is being conveyed, and you remember it too, you must evaluate the message as to what exactly it is conveying to you and how can you use that knowledge in your career. Do not proceed without evaluating the message.

- **Responding** – You must respond appropriately. *Do not*

*complete the speaker's sentence* and learn to *address the speaker's point.* How you respond to a point also indicates if you have been listening properly. Even asking an intelligent question at an appropriate time is listening.

## SILENCE

Not many of us appreciate the value of silence in our conversation. Silence speaks volumes both in the case of the speaker as well on the part of the listener. While the teacher is delivering a lesson, all the students have to stay silent because it allows the teacher to complete the lesson. It also allows everyone else in the class to listen to the teacher and comprehend what is being said. Silence is respecting the speaker and you can break it only once have a need to clarify a point that is of universal importance.

Similarly, for a teacher, to give a pause in-between helps to judge if the students are comfortable with the lesson. Give the student a breather to pause and think before going further.

So, silence is equally important for the speaker and the audience in communication.

Now, having covered the three components of the personality – Appearance, Behavior, and Communication - you would have noticed that you can develop your personality by learning these three components, imbibing them and making these your own. After all, the way you communicate spells volumes of your personality.

*Personality Precedes Person!*

9

# I LIKE! HE/SHE LIKES! WE ALL LIKE!

## INTERPERSONAL SKILLS

*"No matter how educated, talented, rich or cool you believe you are – how you treat people ultimately tells all!"*
*- Anonymous*

A significant part of our days is spent interacting with other fellow beings. When your parents wake you up in the morning, you interact as a parent and a child. It could be in the form of a verbal "good morning", maybe a hug, or just a pleasant touch on your forehead or the cheek. In this relation, love and affection is the strong emotion within you which is being displayed.

You step out of the house, you meet and greet your neighbors, both young and old. This is a friendly stroke, important for respecting fellow beings. This is a "respecting" interaction.

You go to the school/college, meet your class friends, exchange pleasantries, have a laugh, you are interacting in a friendly manner, another emotion – being friendly - is displayed.

You meet and greet the teachers and other seniors in the school/ college, you say "good morning" and/or bow your head in greeting, and this is yet another emotion of respect that comes into play.

These are just some of the examples to state that you interact with other persons, and depending upon the relationship, the situation, your mental built up, your conditioned reflex to a situation, make a part of *interpersonal relationship*.

Interpersonal skills are the behavior and tactics a person uses to interact with others effectively. For the students, the term refers to the student's ability to work well with the parents, teachers, school/college authorities and fellow students with complete understanding. Interpersonal skills range from communication, listening, to attitude, and deportment.

## THREE ELEMENTS OF INTERPERSONAL SKILL

1.   Verbal Communication.

2.   Non-verbal Communication.

3.   Relationship.

From the above examples, you must have noticed that the elements that play an important role in Interpersonal Relationship building are those mentioned above. Let us have a look at these three elements to understand their importance better.

**1. Verbal Communication:** Though, as per Albert Mehrabian, verbal communication constitutes 45% of the process of communication. However, of these, 7% are the words and 38% are the pitch, tone, speed of the spoken word, that are crucial for building up the interpersonal relationship. The choice of words is very important as also the way the words are spoken;

*WHAT* is being spoken is as important as to *HOW* it is spoken. Communication can be by way of questioning and listening. The spoken word is as important as the art of listening between all the participants in this interpersonal relationship.

**2. Non-verbal Communication:** When you see a person for the first time, you form a certain image about the person – as a likable person, wise person, confident person, trustworthy person, etc. depending upon the person's body language. The smile on the face, hand gestures, eye-contact, facial expression, the way the person walks, talks, proximity, that positive stroke that you get from your parents or teachers when you do well, etc., all are parts of the non-verbal communication and it sets the tone of the interpersonal relationship in time to come.

**3. Relationship:** This depends upon various factors like the age, the relationship with you, the position and the situation in which you meet the person. To be successful in life, you need to develop a *healthy relationship* with all the persons you deal with. Even when you differ with the person, you can do so with respect. In other words, it has to be a collaborative relationship for it to last for long with a win-win situation.

The constituents of a *healthy relationship* are

**1. Respect**

You need to respect all the relationships. You show respect to the elders because of age, their wisdom; to the teachers for their role as your teachers giving value to your education; your classmates for being there with you as your friends in need; to others in the family as your family members – mother for being a mother, father for being a father, siblings for being your brother/sister, etc. You show respect to even the strangers you meet by chance. This respect is built up based on the following:

- **Accountability:** Admitting mistakes when wrong, accepting responsibility for the behavior irrespective of the age or any other demographic difference, and respecting others' values and attitudes.

- **Safety:** Allowing the other person to feel safe with you. You do not intimidate the other person due to your superior strength - physical, mental or financial. It also includes expressing yourself in a non-violent way and giving protection to someone who has taken refuge with you.

- **Honesty:** The relationship should be based on honesty. You communicate openly and truthfully, do not look for benefits for yourself at the cost of others, and deal transparently.

- **Kindness:** You have to be kind to others. It goes both ways in the interpersonal relationship. That shows how much you care for each other. This becomes a support system for each other. That's the attitude of compassion.

- **Politeness:** Being polite has always won the day for a person. This also helps the other person to relax and react more positively to you. This also gets reflected in the other person's behavior.

- **Support:** You are there for each other. You support each other's values and beliefs. You understand each other.

> You offer encouragement to each other. You listen to each other and do not become judgmental, thus respecting the other's opinion.

- **Cooperation:** This includes win-win resolution to conflict, asking, not expecting, making decisions together, willing to compromise, and accepting the differences.

- **Trust:** Most important element of interpersonal relationships is developing trust. Being there for the others without questioning, accepting each other's word and standing by the person irrespective of the situation.

Respect is a very important skill to develop. Let's look at its importance from the following quote from Richard Denny:

*"Success, as we all know, comes from people. Outstanding success is very rarely, if ever, achieved by the individual alone. It is achieved with the support, guidance, cooperation advice, willingness, and commitment of others, as well as the individual. How often we see at the awards ceremonies people receiving the award go into thanking others for their help?"*

This means that we all need each other. We all need to understand the dynamics of Interpersonal Skills.

According to a Management Study Guide, *"A strong bond between two or more people refers to interpersonal relationships."*

It is a prerequisite for teamwork and effective execution of any assignment, exhibiting interpersonal skills.

- Individuals in an interpersonal relationship must share

common goals and objectives.

- They should have more or less similar interests and think on the same lines.

- It is always better that the individuals come from similar backgrounds. (However, this may not be possible in most occasions and situations.)

- Individuals in an interpersonal relationship must respect each other's views and opinions. A sense of trust is important.

- Transparency plays a pivotal role in the interpersonal relationship. It is important for an individual to be honest and transparent.

No matter how hard you work or how many brilliant ideas you may have, if you can't connect with people who work around you, your professional life will suffer.

Here, it is important for students to understand the *importance of interpersonal skills* for which I wish to quote Mr. M. Jagran Josh of U.P. Board in his words as follows:

1. It helps them to *ask their doubts* from the teachers and learn better.

2. Helps in building *good relationships* with the peer group, teachers, family members, and society.

3. Boosts their *confidence* and personality development.

4. Helps them express their thoughts, ideas and feelings

> to their parents, teachers, or their classmates to get *help/
> support.*

5. Improves *social status* as they interact and entertain their friends and acquaintances.

6. It helps them *value diversity, individual respect, and different customs* in the society.

7. With better soft skills, a person is considered more *ethical* and gets *respect in society.*

**Conclusion:** Students' interpersonal skills not only help them in their education/school/college life but throughout their **careers** too. As students develop their interpersonal skills during school/college, it becomes a part of their behavior and helps them interact with people from different sectors. Employers too consider students' interpersonal skills as an important factor in selecting a candidate. Hence, interpersonal skills increase chances of employability and a successful career and life."

Another way of understanding the interpersonal skill is by following Eric Berne's **Life Positions**[8].

Berne believes that everyone is born in the same life position.

***I'm not OK, You're OK.***

The reason you are not OK when you are born is because you are dependent on others for all your needs.

They are OK because they can satisfy their own needs and your needs.

[8] Adapted from Image Consulting and Business Institute (ICBI) course material

## What it means?

- "Life Position" refers to the general feeling about life (specifically, the unconscious feeling as opposed to conscious philosophical position) that colors every person to person interaction. There are four such life positions.

  - I'm not OK, You're OK

  - I'm not OK, You're not OK

  - I'm OK, You're not OK

  - I'm OK, You're OK

## What is OKness?

As per Theodore Novey, OKness means,

*"I am an acceptable human being with the right to live and meet my needs and you are an acceptable human being with the right to live and get your needs met."*

- Harris saw OKness almost as a comparison of strength, power, and dependency between a child and his or her parents.

- Stewart and Joines define the degree of OKness a person feels relates to the value he or she feels about self and others.

Let us look at these life positions a little more closely.

**I am not OK, You are OK** (Depressive)

- Feeling powerless, depressed, and inferior.

- Self-deprecating and readily accepts criticism and negative strokes from others.

- Cannot accept the positive strokes easily. Will discount the positive strokes by saying, "No, I could have done better." Or, "I don't think that I look as good as you describe me."

- *It leads to an attitude of depression, powerlessness, and inferiority and thinking that others are better.*

**I am not OK, You are not OK** (Futile)

- It is a black outlook.

- Fortunately, not frequently encountered.

- If a person demonstrates this image for a long time, he is likely to show extreme apathy and will not be productive. *A position of thorough hopelessness and despair.*

**I am OK, You are not OK** (Paranoid)

- I am better and you are no good.

- Attitude of superiority and distrust.

- Operating from a critical and also nurturing parent ego state.

As a realistic assessment, it means that in my opinion *such a person comes over as distrustful, arrogant, and superior who thinks that the others are inferior.*

**I am OK, You are OK** (Good life)

- Healthy, optimistic, and confident attitude towards self and others.

- As a realistic assessment, it means that in my opinion, I am OK despite my deficiencies. I will neither punish myself for these deficiencies, nor totally will I ignore their existence.

- Other people too have deficiencies, but this does not mean that they are second class citizens and cannot be trusted.

*A person accepts others despite their shortcomings and feels OK about himself despite not being perfect.*

Conflicts and criticism tackled from this life position aim to achieve results with an underlying message that I care considerably about you to argue, fight, with you rather than criticize you to belittle you.

*This is the best life position to aim for in interpersonal relationships.*

I advise students to learn about the Life Positions in more detail for understanding interpersonal relationships.

*Suggested reading:*

Equally important to read **Myers Brigs** PERSONALITY TYPES, along with **Johari Window** for in-depth knowledge about interpersonal skills. It will help you to understand and effectively deal with fellow human beings.

10

# THE FEEL FACTOR AND COGNITIVE FACTORS FOR SUCCESS

## THE WORLD OF QUOTIENTS

*"Smart means having intellectual humility rather than high cognitive ability."*
*- Tara Estacaan*

### QUOTIENT

Happiness quotient, Reliability quotient, Employability quotient, Intelligence quotient, Passion quotient, Curiosity quotient; I could go on with the quotients that have been studied and discussed over the recent times. Quotients become a guiding factor for the recruiters and the managers while assessing the human resource – the fellow workers. So, all students should understand and start developing the quotients – it's both felt and is also a cognitive factor.

The word 'quotient' is used when indicating the presence or degree of a characteristic in someone or something.

While researching for various soft skills, various researchers came up with different quotients to explain the soft skills developed in the person or a group of persons under study. If they were studying the measure for academic achievements, they found the intelligence quotient (IQ) as a measure for judging a person's latent capabilities; while studying the interpersonal relationship, they came up with the emotional intelligence and its measure as the EQ (Emotional Quotient.) Once these were understood well, there came the next step of studying the effect of the combinations of the quotients. For instance, while studying the best traits in a would-be employee, Stephen Covey came up with an equation;

$$PQ + CQ > IQ.$$

This is explained as a person with Passion Quotient and Curiosity Quotient will do better than the one who only claims to have a better IQ. At work, it's the passion and the curiosity quotient which are more important for delivering the results, so, the recruiters started looking for persons high on *passion and curiosity quotients* than the person with only the academic achievements – IQ.

All of these quotients have been studied well now and are considered as a very important part for the students to develop as a skill to succeed in life. You may use these in your SWOT analysis. Having the right quotients will go as your strength and the lack of it as a weakness.

Let's understand some of these, one-by-one. These are randomly arranged and not as per their importance as all are important.

**IQ:** *Intelligence quotient* is definitely the first of the quotients studied in relation to measuring the level of intelligence in the students, and later in the employees that you want to recruit. So, it has a direct bearing on building trust in your capability and also your employability. Though based on the academic achievements and the hard skills, it manifests itself in your ability to bring those academic achievements to the workplace. Your understanding of the process, your understanding of implementing the SOP's (Standard Operating Procedures), which is purely an academic exercise, etc., helps you to do your work in the workplace. Later on, you will learn as to what are the other factors, combined with your IQ, which helps you to be more effective at work.

**EQ:** *Emotional quotient,* emotions play a big role in your personality. Hence, you need to develop your emotional intelligence while growing. In fact, it is emotional intelligence which starts building in your personality right from your childhood which, later in your life, will help you to be a good team member and a good social person to be successful in life. It is based on the experiences you have during your early years. Initially, you copy these from your parents, grandparents and your siblings. You learn to act and react to a situation. Your parents show you love and affection, you learn to love them back in return. In your family, everyone talks politely, you make this a part of your personality. You learn to control your anger, and you learn to win friends and build relationships. All this comes from EQ. All those who grow up in an unruly environment, become the misfits of society, the Bullies.

**PQ:** *Passion quotient.* Have you noticed how you approach a certain task during the day? Some tasks you do because you have to do and you cannot avoid, whereas there are other tasks which you love doing! You show a certain amount of enthusiasm and you immerse yourself into these tasks because you are passionate about them. That's why the commercial world looks for a *passion quotient* in a would-be employee. Rightly so, it will determine how an employee will enjoy working on the floor. How much enthusiasm is brought to work; this will decide the work attitude of a person. Coupled with IQ, this helps in bringing in the organizational changes, changes in the approach to the job, changes in the workflow, etc. This is a spin-off of the passion quotient of the employee. Earlier, during your study days too, it manifests itself in the way you study a subject. Your enthusiasm is not the same for all the subjects. Certain subjects you enjoy studying and you bring a certain passion for learning the subject with more gratifying results in the exams. This passion then carries on in its application in life. The energy you put into your work and the enthusiasm with which you approach a task are the traits that the recruiters look for in an applicant. This passion is what sets you apart from the others.

**CQ:** *Curiosity quotient.* If as students we did not have a questioning mind, if we did not raise questions like Why, Where, When, What, Who, and How, imagine our world would have remained a single-dimensional world. The curiosity to find out more about anything that you learn, you experience, you witness is what has brought about the development in our world. And who has to be curious to learn? The student in you. Your quest for knowledge opens up more vistas of learning. Every day, there are persons among us who are asking these questions - What lies beyond the black hole in the universe? What are the effects of gamma rays on the human body? How can we survive on the Mars? Which of the planets can have life on it like here on earth? And the curiosity has led to finding solutions to so many of these factors leading to more understanding. Curiosity leads to questions and answers and most of the inventions are the results of the curiosity. First, you question what is before you, then you find the reason why it is as it is, then you wonder what else can be done with this to be a better thought/product/solution? People are still curious about the creator because we still do not know who is our creator? This is the driving force for satisfying our questions, our curiosity to learn more.

**AQ:** *Adversity quotient.* While we are growing up, we are all conscious about the accolades when we succeed. Very rarely, if at all, a child is mentally prepared to face the failure. There is still a stigma attached to failure. Parents berate you, your teachers criticize you, your classmates, maybe other than your best friends, give you up as a failure, etc. However, failure is just the other side of the coin with success on the other side. Without failure, you cannot understand the success or the joy of it. It is also true that as a student, we are generally protected by our parents against all the adversities of life. Parents do not prepare you for the struggle required in bringing up children with limited means, teachers give extra classes or otherwise give special attention to children with learning difficulties, your friends stand by you in your failure which makes you less ready for adversity. However, you must learn to deal with adversity.

To assess, to plan out solutions to the problem or the cause of the failure, you learn to stay calm in case of an adversity. As a result, you learn to get over it maturely without allowing it to stress you! This intelligence that you develop to deal with adversity is the Adversity quotient – AQ. How you react to the failure, do you panic or take charge of the things, you seek answers to the cause of the failure, you question yourself as to where did you go wrong, and how will you overcome these in the future? If you panic, it means, your AQ is low; you will tend to repeat the mistakes in the future. So, as a student, develop the habit of building your AQ so that you can face adversities better.

**DQ:** *Decency quotient.* In today's world, where we are all interdependent on each other, there is a way of dealing with the things what is known as decency. If a person has not been able to keep the appointment and he calls up to say sorry, we say that he had the *decency* to inform us. You speak politely to a person who has just spilled your coffee, that's a decent way of handling the situation. A student walks up to the teacher and apologizes to the teacher that the homework is not done, the teacher smiles back and suggest how to do it at the earliest and submit to the teacher. The student will remember the teacher as a very decent person. There are hundreds of examples in your daily life that will set you apart as a decent person if you show respect and care for the other person. This is the bedrock of your interpersonal relationship. You go through the day with a happiness quotient, making life more comfortable for everyone, you win the trust of the others, and you get better at negotiation with others and have a win-win situation because of your decency; so why will you not work on the Decency Quotient in your life? Simple words like please, thank you, I am sorry, if I may, etc. if sincerely practiced in your life are the indicators of your *decency quotient.*

**OQ:** *Open quotient.* As we have discussed and understood earlier that we have to work in a team these days. There are very few things in life today that we do outside of a team. Also, very little is achieved by being rigid about *your* way of doing things. You have to be open about it and accept other's point of view also. To be collaborative, connecting with your team members well, you have to have an open mind. Listen to the other person's suggestions; deliberate on it, again, with an open mind. This is how you demonstrate your decency – *Open Decency.*

An open mind is an open window for knowledge to breeze in. You learn more by being open about life experiences. By experience, you learn more. If you stay in a groove and not peep out, there are all the possibilities that you miss the opportunities life has to offer to gain knowledge.

**SQ:** *Spiritual quotient.* It is often quoted "when everything fails, faith prevails." This is one trust in your life which helps you to deal with so many difficult situations. To my mind, we must follow the path of spirituality. I do not mean the blind faith of the religious kind. You must have faith in your creator. You must be grateful for what HE provides to us. You must be thankful to HIM for the knowledge gained. Spirituality means the knowledge about your inner self gained by introversion. Looking at the world around you as a school/college of learning, taking the messages of our spiritual gurus, everyone has stated, "be kind to the others," "be generous," "respect others and their beliefs," and in turn, practice the same in your life. Help others, be tolerant of their values, respect their way of life, etc. This part of the spiritual thought which helps you to deal with other human beings is called the Spiritual Quotient. Do the meditation, detox your mind by following your spiritual guru's teachings; it will help you to deal with your life situations better, in particular in adversity.

**EMPLOYABILITY QUOTIENT:** The whole book is dedicated to help students understand the soft skills and the benefits thereof. The whole purpose is to help students succeed at whatever they wish to pursue in their life. In a way, this helps the students to increase their *Employability Quotient!*

Employability Quotient is the ability to do better at whatever task you undertake and doing it with more efficiency and more effectively as compared to others. When you demonstrate soft-skills at the time of the interview, the interviewer looks for certain qualities, like all the quotients mentioned above, to gain the confidence in your abilities to do the job better more skillfully than the other candidates, and your chances of being hired to go up many folds. Isn't that what we are looking to achieve by acquiring these skills?

Work on these **Quotients** to achieve success in life.

# Conclusion

While concluding my book - The Winning Deal – I wish to state that this is a sincere effort on the part of the author to apprise the readers about the need for the soft skills and the advantages thereof.

I am sure, while reading the book, you would have realized that, YES, there is a need for acquiring soft-skills for success in life. Also, that it is not so difficult to work on your self-development. Step-by-step, skill-by-skill, you can achieve so much more and remain ahead of your peers. That is, learning to move toward our goals and desires one step at a time, often just one baby-step at a time, and learning to love the doing, learning to use the accumulation of time. When we multiply tiny pieces of time with small increments of daily effort, we too will find we can accomplish magnificent things. We can change ourselves.

All that you need to do now is to follow the suggestions given by the author, for acquiring the skills, one-by-one, work on the suggested lines and let these become your habits. Good habits will lead to a great behavior; a wonderful personality; and will build up your acceptability, both at home and work.

That's **THE WINNING DEAL!**

# Acknowledgment

First and foremost, this is my first book at 79+ years! Readers may find my acknowledgment a little awkward because that's the way I am feeling, showing my gratitude to hundreds of people who have influenced my thoughts and my life till now, and some of them continue to do so; it remains 'work in progress.' It is not possible for me to name all the persons who have walked with me and influenced my thought-process; however, I must acknowledge the contribution of a few who have/and mean a lot to me.

Above all, God, guiding, hand-holding, protecting me through all the ups and downs in my life, and for teaching me the life's lessons which one can never learn otherwise. This continues to add to my learning curve. Learning is not age-barred.

Then, I wish to thank my parents and my mother-in-law, who, in their way, taught me to deal with anything that was thrown at us as a family and deal with the same, upholding the belief in myself and also maintaining self-esteem. They built up my personality based on a strong character-building – a sense of family values, integrity, honesty, and love for our country. From them, I learned the art of keeping the family together, and sharing with love and affection.

I learned the lesson in Interpersonal and Intrapersonal skills from my parents and my mother-in-law. Can you learn it any other way?

I am grateful to my wife, Asha, who stood by me always, stoically supporting me, with the unflinching faith in me. Thanks to her that I learned the lesson of staying confident and walk with my head held high.

My three sons, Rahul, Rajat, and Ritesh and then, in turn their spouses, Ashima, Sunaina, and Ekata respectively, and my five loving grandchildren, Gayatri, Kabir, Khushi, Kartik, and Saachi, who gave me the lessons in love and affection, never questioning me even when I, at times, may have failed as a parent and/or as a grandparent. In fact, they have contributed tremendously to my cognitive thoughts. I simply had to observe them growing, accepting the challenges attached to their growing up, their achievements, and very rarely, some setbacks which were always very temporary. This added to my emotional intelligence which is so important for understanding life.

My family at large, both on my side as well as on my wife's side – these are institutions in themselves. I learned the art of accepting everyone on their merits, we never saw anything negative in anyone else. Standing by the family in case of sorrow and enjoying life to the hilt, celebrating the joyous landmarks like births & marriages; achievements of the family members, etc. This added to the positivity in my life and helped in moving on without thinking about the negativity in any way. What a contribution to the rich experience that I can share with others, now!

I am not forgetting the influence my school/college teachers had on me. ALL of them held me by the hand and taught the art of growing up - the discipline, the etiquette, the hard work, taking the academic lessons as seriously as the life's lessons mentioned above, honesty, patience, respect for others, being a team member, etc. which are difficult to learn otherwise. I wish to acknowledge their contribution by saying a big thank-you to all of them. This is strongly reflected in my book while writing about these soft-skills.

I was very fortunate that the first job I landed after graduation, I started working under a guru, Mr. K. C. Dhanda. (I love to remember him as KCD!) His nuggets of wisdom have become part of my cognitive thoughts and influence my thinking and my behavior till now. The passion and the verve with which he went through his day, taught me to take life as it comes; yet be ready for any challenges. He never buckled in the face of challenges, always giving/sharing, advising all the youngsters coming in touch with him. He was a great teacher, mentor, benefactor for so many of us. Not many can claim of sharing their knowledge and wisdom as freely as KCD. He encouraged my habit of reading, in fact, introduced me to some of the authors, and I am grateful to him for that.

The real urge for writing this book came from my years, mentoring, CD Foundation of Education school in Dharuhera. During the years, I have interacted with the school authorities, teachers, students, and at times, with the parents as well, at this school has taught me skills I possess, in a big way. I have developed empathy, understanding the children in all their avatars, as self-centered children to gregarious children, being quiet and introverted to being boisterous and outgoing, etc. I have worked with them during their failures and also celebrated their achievements. I have, in the meanwhile, understood the need for soft-skills for a Winning Deal in their lives.

They, collectively, have inspired me to share my understanding of this all-important aspect of today's growing up. I do hope the readers benefit from it.

Can one forget one's alma mater? I learned all my soft-skills presentations from Image Consulting and Business Institute (ICBI), Gurugram, with H.O. in Mumbai. I am grateful to the promoters, Mr. Rakesh Agarwal and Ms. Suman Agarwal, and the trainers at ICBI for providing me the opportunity to hone my skills. I have to specially mention Mr. Shyam Kumar and Ms. Sangeeta Singh for very informative sessions going through the "Train The Trainer" learning. I am grateful to all my fellow learners at TTT sessions, who have all helped me to understand the need for soft skills for students in particular. In fact, my writing on the subject is strongly influenced by what I was taught at ICBI, hence, at times, I have used the knowledge so gained at ICBI in various chapters. This learning, coupled with my life-time experience, added to my understanding the finer nuances of the skills I already possessed. My readers should join me in thanking the ICBI for the knowledge I share with them through this book. I accept some of my thoughts will be mirroring their thoughts. This I wish to say as a compliment to ICBI and all of my teachers at ICBI.

Finally, my habit of reading inculcated very early in my life. Starting with The Children's Digest, The Readers Digest, TIME magazine, The Illustrated Weekly of India, etc. and a whole lot of comics available in the early '50s. Then, I graduated to reading books on various subjects. The essence of all the books I have read until now is remarkably coming out in my writing. Starting with Pearl S. Buck, Leo Tolstoy, Maxim Gorky, Mulkh Raj Anand, Jawahar Lal Nehru, Mahatma Gandhi, and then Peter Drucker, Phillip Kotler, Eric Berne, to more recently the likes of Brian Tracy, Zig Ziglar, Stephen Covey, John C. Maxwell and many more. I am surely not forgetting Dr. A. P. J. Abdul Kalam, our ex-president, and a great scientist. He is my icon! The way he has interacted, guided, and influenced children in our country is worth emulating. His thoughts, too, are reflected in my writing; hence, I am grateful to him. There, at times, will be knowledge shared in my book, inadvertently not giving the reference to the rightful source, it is only because of the fact that I may have been using that knowledge for so long that it has become a part of my cognitive thoughts, without realizing the mistake. I wish to be pardoned for the same.

In the end, I wish to state, that makes me not the only author of this book. It's the collective thoughts of so many others I came in touch with, personally or through their books, and I am only the conduit and I am grateful to all of them for making me the sutradhār.

**V. N. Kashyap**

authorvnkashyap@gmail.com

www.ingramcontent.com/pod-product-compliance
Lightning Source LLC
Chambersburg PA
CBHW051448130726
47987CB00005B/2231